Handbook for SPIRITUAL GROWTH

A Guide for Catholics

· · · · · · · · · · · · · ·

PHILIP ST. ROMAIN

LIGUORI
PUBLICATIONS

One Liguori Drive
Liguori, MO 63057-9999
(314) 464-2500

Imprimi Potest:
James Shea, C.SS.R.
Provincial, St. Louis Province
The Redemptorists

Imprimatur:
+ Edward J. O'Donnell, D.D.
Archdiocese Administrator, Archdiocese of St. Louis

ISBN 0-89243-541-0
Library of Congress Catalog Card Number: 93-78436

Scripture quotations are taken from the NEW AMERICAN BIBLE WITH REVISED NEW TESTAMENT, copyright © 1986, AND THE REVISED PSALMS, copyright © 1991, by the Confraternity of Christian Doctrine, 3211 Fourth Street, N.E., Washington, D.C., and are used with permission. All rights reserved.

The excerpt from *The Method of Centering Prayer* by Thomas Keating is used with permission of Contemplative Outreach, Ltd., Butler, New Jersey.

The excerpt from "So Our Souls Can Catch Up" originally appeared in *Praying* magazinge, January-February 1993.

Steps Eight and Nine (on pages 58 and 59) of the Twelve Steps are reprinted with permission of Alcoholics Anonymous World Services, Inc. Permission to reprint and adapt the Twelve Steps does not mean that AA agrees with the views expressed herein. AA is a program of recovery from alcoholism. Use of the Twelve Steps in connection with programs and activities which are patterned after AA but which address other problems does not imply otherwise.

Cover design by Chris Sharp

Contents

Foreword

We are a spiritual people.

The truth of this statement may be discovered by reflecting on the experience of being human.

Is it not true that we yearn for fulfillment, for an answer to the question "What is it all about?" Doesn't there seem to be within us a certain emptiness, a certain hunger, that cannot be easily filled?

Such questions, and others that flow from deep within us in moments of reflection, meditation, or sometimes even just exhaustion, are reflective of a core spiritual nature within the human person. The search for answers to these questions leads us on what might be understood as a journey. When we put the two experiences together, we discover that each of us is a spiritual person on a spiritual journey.

My own experiences of being human and of being on a spiritual journey have led me to conclude that, for whatever reason, we are created in this way or—if not created—we became this way through choice and decision. It may not have always been through our own personal choices and decisions but possibly through a corporate, original choice and decision. (See Genesis 3:1-19.) This journeying, questioning self seems to have something to do with who we are.

If you find yourself in some agreement with the experiences

I have described, if you have discovered yourself faced with the experience of "needing to be filled," then you may also resonate with the experience of trying all sorts of different paths, seeking to be filled.

Each of us journey in different ways. We make a series of choices and decisions, believing that somehow we may discover something or someone that will fill us. This pattern, this experience, is nothing to be ashamed of, nothing to run from or deny. It seems to be pretty normal to the human experience.

The first place we usually turn to be filled is to the material world. We assume that the hunger within us is a hunger that can be filled with "stuff," and so we begin the process of accumulating.

At first, accumulation does seem to satisfy us. However, as time goes on we discover that the stuff of life just doesn't seem to do it for us. There doesn't seem to be enough stuff—enough money, enough relationships—to fill us and make us whole. In a moment of honesty, we might admit that all we have succeeded in doing is to distract ourselves, to take a detour on our journey. But we haven't begun to deal with the real issue at hand.

It is only after this initial experience, this false start, if you will, that we are really able to begin the journey.

It is at this point in your journey that you will find the *Handbook for Spiritual Growth* to be useful and important.

When you begin a journey, it is important to have a map or a guide or someone who can lead you and point you in the right direction. A good guide is essential, and a good guide is someone who actually has been where you want to go and who knows how to show the way.

Philip St. Romain is such a person. He is the author of books and articles on the spiritual life, a popular retreat director, and—most important of all—a practitioner of what he teaches.

I had the privilege of working with Philip at the Spiritual Life Center in Wichita, Kansas. As we worked together designing retreats and programs for spiritual growth, I was continually impressed with his personal dedication to prayer, contemplation, and the spiritual journey. He spoke with authority about the many different paths, methods, and models of which he writes in this handbook. I have always found him to be a truthful guide and a helpful friend.

Enjoy your journey, trust your guide, and discover the way that will lead you to be truly human.

Rev. Thomas M. Santa, C.SS.R.
President
Liguori Publications

PART ONE

The Essence of Christian Spirituality

Introduction

Christian spirituality is a topic about which volumes have been written by many different authors. Any single aspect of Christian spirituality, such as its history or its various modes of expression, could involve hundreds of pages of reflection and documentation.

However, I am presenting here a brief sketch of what I call the essence of Christian spirituality. In using the term *essence,* I am referring to what is at the heart of all the various forms of Christian spirituality—monastic, clerical, religious, lay, and other. Although these various spiritualities embody different lifestyles, they all do so out of a common center of faith and concern. Once we grasp this center, we can easily see how Christian spirituality differs from other, non-Christian spiritualities. We can also begin to discern our own individual and unique manner of expressing the spiritual life.

The material in Part One is broken into several subtopics, each of which offers some insight into Christian spirituality. The material is presented in outline form, rather than in short essays, to stimulate the reader to make his or her own intuitive reflections. The outline form also allows for a quick review of the material from time to time.

We conclude Part One with a discussion of the "work" of Christian spirituality. The chapters which follow will include resources for study and reflection to encourage and support us in this "work."

What Is Spirituality?

To understand what spirituality is, let us compare it with two similar but not identical concerns: religion and morality.

Religion: Religion is a *living tradition of wisdom* and *worship.*

- *Living* means that there are people who practice this religion. It is not merely found in a book. It is a community of believers.
- *Tradition* refers to a body of truth passed on from one generation to the next through written and other means.
- *Wisdom* describes teachings that point out the relation-

ship between human beings and the Divine and how to live out this relationship.

- *Worship* is the rituals and other means to celebrate the relationship with the Divine, both individually and communally.

Morality: Morality is the *practice* of *behavioral principles* for conduct which further the *common good*.

- *Practice* is a repeated effort to do something.
- *Behavioral principles* are values that encourage certain behaviors while discouraging others.
- *Common good* is the goal toward which moral behavior tends. This, of course, is defined in many different ways.

Spirituality: Spirituality is *a way of life* that ensues from a particular *center of meaning and value*, bringing a particular quality of *energy* and *awareness* to the one who follows this way of life.

- *A way of life* is the manner in which one actually lives, one's lifestyle.
- *Center of meaning and value* is what one lives for. What is of most importance or of ultimate concern?
- *Energy* is the quality of aliveness in an individual's life, the power to do something.
- *Awareness* pertains to one's alertness and perception. How one sees things, what is seen, and "who" sees.

The Relationship Between Spirituality, Religion, and Morality

1. *It is possible to be moral without being especially religious or spiritual.* Such might be the case with an agnostic humanist, who works for the common good but not from any particular religious tradition and without firm allegiance to any particular center of meaning and value.

2. *It is possible to be religious without being spiritual or moral.* Such religiosity characterized many of the scribes and the Pharisees of Jesus' time. In such cases, which continue to abound in this age, one could be familiar with the tradition and participating in its rituals but not be committed to living out a particular center of meaning and value. In fact, attachment to religious dogmas and rituals could be an obstacle to spirituality for some.

3. *It is possible to live spiritually without being committed to any particular religion.* Many people are doing so in this day. They generally believe in a good and loving God but pledge no allegiance to any particular religion and worship with no community. Frequently, they are ecclectic in their beliefs about God, picking and choosing from various religions. They are living a spirituality, however, in that they honestly try to center their lives and motives in these truths.

4. *It is impossible to live a spiritual life without living a moral life.* Any authentic center of meaning and value ought to encourage behavior unto the common good. Hence, spirituality is of a higher level of concern than morality, and morality is foundational to spirituality.

5. Although one can be spiritual without being religious, *it is far better if a spirituality is informed by a religious body of truth,*

supported by a community of believers, and celebrated ritually. Without religion, spirituality can easily lose its focus, becoming too ecclectic, too ecumenical, and too soft-headed.

6. *Ideally, religion ought to be the means by which people embrace the moral life and enter into the spiritual journey.* Religion issues the invitation to the moral and spiritual life and provides the tools, wisdom, and support for living this life.

What's "Christian" About Christian Spirituality?

As with all spiritualities, Christian spirituality is a way of life ensuing from a particular center of meaning and value, bringing a particular energy and awareness to those who practice this way of life. This center and its implications are given focus by the Christian religion and its unique understanding of the Divine.

Centeredness: In the Christian religion, centeredness is focused in Jesus Christ, who is the giver of the indwelling Spirit and who is the way to the transcendent Father. Hence, Christian spirituality is a Trinitarian spirituality. Jesus is not to be worshiped to the exclusion of the Father and the Spirit. To overemphasize or underemphasize devotion to any of the Persons of the Trinity would be to lose the kind of centeredness Christian spirituality invites.

Way of Life: Christian spirituality aims to take seriously Jesus' call to follow him. Christian spirituality is the individual's effort to make the life of Christ visible in his or her unique situation.

Energy: The energy that characterizes the Christian is love for God, the human community, and indeed, all of creation. This love moves in the direction of creating a human community which images the love of the Trinity and a planetary harmony which images the harmony and peace of heaven.

Awareness: Christianity sees the whole of creation as the work of God. Consequently, Christian spirituality is alert to the goodness of God revealed in the human heart, in creation, and in all of history. Christian spirituality is interested in the events of the day. It does not reject the world as illusory or human affairs as an obstacle to spiritual growth.

Three Types of Christian Spirituality

All Christian spiritualities have in common the characteristics listed in the previous pages. Nevertheless, there are three general "ways of life" that attempt to express the meaning of Christ. In their book *Ignation Spirituality and the Directed Retreatant*, Sister Judith Roemer and Reverend George Schemel, S.J., describe these three ways as discussed below. Each has a long and rich history. The resources in this handbook are designed to serve the needs of people living out of an Apostolic Spirituality.

Monastic Spirituality
- *Examples:* Carthusians, Trappists, Benedictines, Cistercians
- *Style of life:* Regular, simple, ascetical, familial
- *Tonality:* Flight from the world
- *Involvement with the world:* Little; only with those who come to them

- *Organization:* Hierarchical-familial
- *Apostolate:* One of testimony; a witness of faith
- *Prayer:* Divine Office; Prayer of the Hours

Psychological-Contemplative Spirituality

- *Examples:* Carmelites, Poor Clares, Dominicans, Passionists, Charismatics
- *Style of life:* Regular, familial, not as simple and ascetical as monastic
- *Tonality:* "We have not here a lasting city."
- *Involvement with the world:* Very limited
- *Organization:* Familial-hierarchical
- *Apostolate:* More involved with people than the monastic but primarily through the ministry of prayer
- *Prayer:* Liturgy of the Hours; private contemplation

Apostolic Spirituality

- *Examples:* Laypeople, diocesan priests, Redemptorists, Jesuits, many religious orders
- *Style of life:* Irregular; complex; not as ascetical/familial
- *Tonality:* Incarnational; great involvement with the world
- *Involvement with the world:* Very much "in" the world, but not "of" the world
- *Organization:* Discerning-professional; many different kinds of organizational patterns
- *Apostolate:* Direct; involved; incarnational; transforming the world into the kingdom of God
- *Prayer:* Not much emphasis on Liturgy of the Hours, more on private prayer/contemplation, self-knowledge, "finding God in all things," prayer encompassing daily living

The "Work" of
Christian Spirituality

In order to live a life imaging the love of Christ, we must transform everything within ourselves that moves in a contrary direction. This calls for hard work, perseverance, and plenty of prayer.

The hard work might be summarized under the following goals, each of which will be developed more fully in the chapters to come.

Letting go of disordered desires and attachments

"For where your treasure is, there also will your heart be" (Luke 12:34).

If our heart and its desires are centered on worldly and unspiritual concerns, then we need to see this clearly and to establish new priorities. The false self in each of us is the source of our disordered desires.

Centering our lives in God through Christ

"Therefore, you shall love the LORD, your God, with all your heart, and with all your soul, and with all your strength" (Deuteronomy 6:5).

A spiritually centered person loves God above all and seeks to have his or her will conformed to the will of God. In giving up disordered attachments, it becomes possible to begin growing in faith.

Healing and reconciliation

"...and forgive us our debts, as we forgive our debtors" (Matthew 6:12).

We must let go of all resentment, shame, and anxious preoccupation. These keep us bound to the past and allow the false self to make a claim on the will.

Changing old attitudes

Do not conform yourself to this age but be transformed by the renewal of your mind, that you may discern what is the will of God, what is good and pleasing and perfect (Romans 12:2).

If we are to remain free from negative emotions and peaceful in the present moment, we must change the way we think about ourselves, other people, creation, and God's will.

Living Daily

"Do not worry about tomorrow; tomorrow will take care of itself. Sufficient for a day is its own evil" (Matthew 6:34).

We learn to live one day at a time, doing each day what must be done, learning from the past, hoping in the future. We also learn to meet our own needs in a new way, without the complications of the false self.

PART TWO

· · · · · · · · · · · · · · · · ·

Our Broken Human Condition

In Part Two we focus on the human condition, calling special attention to the issue of centeredness and how we have lost our centeredness in God. Individual entries in Part Two are arranged topically and are not meant to suggest a sequence for doing spiritual work. Therefore, while I suggest that you read this section and begin working some of the exercises, I urge you also to jump ahead to Part Three, "Centering Your Heart in God's Care," especially to the section on prayer (if you do not already have a regular life of prayer).

The Spiritual Nature
of Human Consciousness

There are many ways to speak of human consciousness. We are concerned here with identifying its spiritual nature. With this purpose in mind, we can define consciousness as attention itself.

What is attention? One is reminded of Saint Augustine's response to the question "What is time?" He said, "When you do not ask me, I know; but when you ask me, I don't know."

Attention is like that. We know *that* it is, but we don't know exactly *what* it is. It is like a light within that enables us to perceive things outside ourselves and inside ourselves. Attention can be attuned to inner thoughts, memories, and images; it can also perceive through the senses. Yet attention is one thing, and that which is attended to is quite another. When we combine the two, we can speak of *states of consciousness*. A state of consciousness is attention plus its contents (thoughts, feelings, memories, sense objects). We are always in some kind of state of consciousness; the question is, what kind?

There is a subjective and personal quality about attention. Generally, the light of attention does not shine out like a radar—without focus and in all directions. It is usually focused or directed in some manner. That which focuses attention is the *self*. The self is to attention as a hand is to a flashlight. The light shines where the hand that holds the flashlight directs it to shine, and it is the self that directs the focus of attention.

From the foregoing, we can conclude that the self is at the center of attention. It is the *chooser* implicit in all acts of attention. All of one's thoughts, feelings, memories, desires—the contents of consciousness—are in some way shaped and directed by the intentionality of the self. We know this from experience. If we want to think of something, we can think of it;

if we don't want to think of it, we can push it away (for a short while, at least).

The intentionality, or free will, of the self is not without its limitations, however. We cannot always think what we want to or turn off an unpleasant mood when we want to. Sometimes the contents of consciousness are so loaded with energy that they simply overwhelm the power of free choice. This is the experience of powerlessness, of the inability to direct our lives as we intend.

Why does this happen? We shall learn more about this in the pages ahead. Suffice it to say that there are psychological consequences to the choices we make, and we cannot will these consequences away. For now, we recognize the intentional, or "will-ing," influence of the self and how this intentionality colors our attention.

What is the self intending, or will-ing? The answer (or answers) to this question reveals to us the center of our consciousness. This center, we might say, is the root of our spirituality.

Ego and Self: In speaking of the self as the intentional center of consciousness, we must acknowledge that there are two aspects to the self.

First, there is the conscious self, or *ego*. This is what most people think of as their self. But the ego is not the whole self. The ego is to the self as the self is to attention; the ego is the conscious agent of the self. This ego stands between the outside world and the unconscious inside world as the arbitrating agent between their demands.

The ego is usually identified with *self-image*. What is self-image?

- Self-image is the picture we have of ourselves as a result of our life experiences. When we focus this picture into the realm of thought, we can speak of *self-concept.* Self-concept is our idea of ourselves; self-image is the picture of this idea.

- Self-image/concept arises from...

1. *Groups and labels we are identified with:* American, Catholic, Kansan, Cardinals fan, St. Romain. When someone comments on these groups, we are affected.
2. *Our roles:* mother, husband, brother, counselor, minister, son, and so forth. These roles give us a sense of identity.
3. *Our self-judgments:* pretty, intelligent, tall, stubborn. When someone's opinions conflict with our own self-judgments, we are deeply affected.
4. *Others' judgments:* this may be identical with our own self-judgments, or there may be differences.

Self-image, then, is what gives the ego its form, or structure. The ego makes its choices by referring to self-image. If, for example, a friend asks me to take a ballet class with her, I project my self-image into this possibility. I may say, "I can't see myself doing that." I am saying that the picture I have of myself does not do ballet dancing. When people say, "This is who I am," they are usually referring to self-image.

Although most people identify their ego as their whole self, we know this cannot be true. There are hours and hours of every day when we do not even experience the ego. For example, there is no ego experience when we sleep—except during dreams. Yet we know that a self still exists when we sleep, for if someone calls our name, we wake up. It is a deeper level of self that recognizes our name during sleep. Then it is self that begins to function as ego after we wake up.

We must recognize, therefore, a second aspect of self—an unconscious, nonegoic dimension. The intentionality of this *unconscious self* may be quite a bit different from ego. The unconscious self wants harmony and wholeness for the whole person. What the ego wants might be something altogether different—something that brings the person into disharmony and fragmentation. Hence, we frequently find a conflict between the ego and the unconscious self.

The language of the ego is that of the culture. Dreams, spontaneous fantasies, and intuitive hunches are the language of the unconscious self. It is through such nonverbal language that the unconscious self tries to communicate with the ego.

We have noted that it is the unconscious self that hears and recognizes our name when we sleep. We now note that it is also the unconscious self that knows and recognizes the presence of God. Deep within, this unconscious self is already attuned to the presence of God, for it is God who gives life to the self in each moment. The striving for wholeness by the unconscious self is *"in*-formed," we might say, by its awareness of God. This is not to say, as the Hindus do, that the unconscious self is God, or Atman. God is the One who gives the self its existence. The self is the one who is aware of being given existence by God.

Conditioned for Unhappiness: When we are born, there is no ego. There is only the unconscious self expressing through a limited number of instinctive behaviors. This unconscious self is also attuned to its environment in a feeling way. As infants, we can tell whether we are loved or rejected. As we develop, we are being shaped by environment at the level of emotion. Within a few months, we begin to understand something of the meaning of the words we are hearing. By the age of two, we understand many words, including the words *me* and *mine*. At this stage, the human subject is capable of perceiving himself or herself as an object of attention. This is the beginning of the ego.

In a perfect world, where everyone unconditionally loved everyone else, the ego would exist in a beautiful harmony with the unconscious self. This unconscious self would, in turn, be a medium through which God's presence would always be informing the decisions of the ego. As we all know, this is not the situation in which we find ourselves.

Instead, what we find is disharmony between the concerns of the ego and the deeper self. Consequently, the ego has lost its "natural" sense of God's presence and feels alienated from God. We are more awake to the concerns of ego than to the presence of God, which is a sure sign that something has gone wrong.

How did this happen to us? Here is a hypothetical scenario:

1. The environment in which we grow up loves us conditionally. This begins in the womb, where the developing embryo is attuned to the emotional state of the mother and, through her, to the rest of the world. Later, the care given the infant by the parents and family communicates *conditional love* in many ways.

2. When the embryo and later the infant is loved conditionally, he or she experiences at least a slight sense of rejection and the emotion of fear. If one is loved very little, there is great fear and distrust very deep within.

3. As the ego begins to develop, the emotional consequences of conditional love—mostly fear, distrust, and shame—create a turmoil in the unconscious that prevents the ego from developing in harmony with the unconscious self. It is as though the light of God mediated through the unconscious self is blocked out by these deep emotional scars. Hence, the ego will be much more attuned to the outside world and will be in some kind of avoidance posture toward the inner world of the unconscious as it develops.

4. The ideas and images of ourselves that we pick up from the developmental environment reinforce our feeling of being loved conditionally. In many ways, we learn that we are loved for what we do, not for who we are. At the level of thought,

therefore, we conclude that we are conditionally lovable and acceptable. Our self-judgment and our perception of others' judgments of us—two integral parts of self-image—are deeply colored by this conditionality.

5. Concluding that we are only conditionally lovable and acceptable, we are constantly on the alert for the conditions by which we can become more acceptable to ourselves and others. These conditions are perceived to exist in externals—in the opinions of others, in accomplishments, in money and other possessions. The center of attention of the ego, then, is drawn to the outside world as the source of happiness.

6. Having lost touch with the presence of God in the ground of our deepest self, the ego has also lost its true identity. To compensate, it identifies strongly with family roles, nation, race, athletic heroes, and other people to gain for itself some kind of identity through association.

This, then, is a brief summary of how we become split within ourselves through the experience of conditional love. Since everyone grows up in an environment of conditional love, everyone experiences this kind of brokenness and loss of contact with God. There are a wide range of possibilities here, since some environments are much more loving than others. To the extent that we have not been loved for who we are, however, we are damaged.

The False Self System

Out of this condition of wounding and brokenness, we develop a *false self*. This false self is a whole dimension of the personality, encompassing both egoic and unconscious levels. It is not the whole of the personality, however. Were that so, we would be incapable of seeing the reality of our condition, and we would never be able to change. Nevertheless, the degree of infection by the false self system is very pervasive. It is like a cancer that has spread throughout the entire soul, although it has not completely killed the soul. The deepest, unconscious self-center remains free from contamination by the false self.

What is this false self like? Let us list a few of its characteristics by summarizing its philosophy of life.

- I am conditionally lovable and acceptable. I have no real worth in and of myself. *I must do something to be loved and accepted.* My worth is predicated on doing the right things.
- The conditions for getting love and acceptance are defined by people and circumstances outside myself. Therefore, I must use my rational intelligence to constantly scan the culture and the opinions of others to perceive the conditions by means of which I will attain a sense of worth and meaning. I am constantly judging other people and circumstances according to my perceived conditions for happiness.
- I will do whatever is necessary to gain the approval of others, all the while avoiding their disapproval. I will reveal those aspects of myself to others that I think they want to see; for if they knew what I really thought and felt, they might not accept me.
- The God I believe in is utterly transcendent—totally outside of myself. Like everything else, I have to do certain things the right way in order to gain God's approval. Religion teaches me what these right things are.
- When I feel numb or painful inside as a result of living according to this philosophy, I will use mood-altering "fixes" to make myself feel better or to take the edge off my inner pain.

Anyone can see that this philosophy of life is laden with many pitfalls. Few people are free of this consciousness, however, because as already noted, there are both conscious and unconscious aspects to this false self system. Also, for many people, this false self is so dominant and so caught up in external concerns that they are little aware of anything else.

The false self system is responsible for all our misery and for the destruction of the planet. It is totally out of touch with the harmonizing influences of the deeper self, so it is constantly trying to change the external world and external circumstances in an attempt to gain happiness. Because our happiness is within and is not a consequence of inadequate external factors, the false self only succeeds in creating disharmony in the world. This disharmony has brought the planet to a state of crisis!

Spirituality and the False Self: Working as a system of consciousness at the level of the ego and the unconscious, the false self—like all other states of consciousness—operates out of a certain intentionality, or center. This center, we have noted, is a spiritual issue.

What is the center, or intentionality, of the false self?

It is looking outward to other people, things, or circumstances to make us happy. This is its general orientation, fired by the intellectual and emotional convictions that in and of ourselves we are flawed, a mistake, unlovable, and unacceptable. We think we must accomplish something or get something to be loved, so we are always looking outside ourselves to discover what this might be. We call this external referencing.

Specifically, this external referencing is usually focused on one source as most responsible for our happiness. Most commonly, this is another person. We tell ourselves that we cannot be okay without that person's good opinion of us, without his or her approval, without being special to that person. Sometimes it is not one person but a group of people (maybe the whole world!)

that we are trying to impress. When we do succeed in getting this approval, we feel high, thrilled, exalted! It is like a drug. The more we get, the more we want.

Of course, the shadow side of this is that when they do not give us approval, we feel low, devastated, down on ourselves. As a result of depending on other people in this way for our happiness, we lose the freedom to really be ourselves before others. We are constantly wondering what they think, and our mind is preoccupied with this, draining the psyche of energies that could be used for other purposes.

What I have just described is *relationship addiction*, or *codependency*. It is but one possible manifestation of the false self system. External referencing might also be focused in work, accomplishments, sex, gambling, winning, food, television, alcohol and drugs, shopping, and a wide range of other mood-altering possibilities. Any and all of these can be used addictively and can become full-blown addictions in their own right.

In a real sense, then, the false self system is an addictive self. Here are a few conclusions which force themselves upon us at this point:

1. Addictive fixes are the center on which the false self focuses. Addiction, then, is primarily a spiritual concern. It is the "spirituality" of the false self, giving rise, like all spiritualities, to a particular way of life and bringing a particular quality of energy and awareness to the one who lives this life. This way of life, its energy, and the attentional state it expresses all belong to the false self.
2. Everyone has been loved conditionally and has developed a false self to compensate for this. Only Jesus Christ and his mother, Mary, are excluded from this disease.
3. Everyone is an addict. The question is, what kind? Some, myself included, use a wide variety of things as fixes. Others use only one or two.

4. The false self system with its addictive preoccupations is the primary obstacle to experiencing God's presence.

This is putting the matter quite bluntly, I realize, and few people want to admit that they are addicts. But if we are to grow in Christian spirituality, the truth of the fourth point cannot be overstated. If we would come to center our lives in Christ, then we must also recognize that there is much about us that will resist the changes in lifestyle that Christian spirituality calls for. Let us identify the false self system right from the beginning as the source of this resistance. The false self is that within us that resists Christ. Using other, more theological terms, Saint Paul called it the presence of sin living in himself. (See Romans 7:15-25.)

I am sometimes greatly disturbed by the prevalent attitude that this false self system is "natural." It is *not* natural; it is common, however. God did not create people to become false selves. The false self is a perversion of what God has created. Its centers of meaning and value have nothing to do with God's will.

In the following pages, you will be invited to get in touch with the presence of this false self in your own life. The purpose of these exercises is not to get you down on yourself but to help you begin to see the false self for what it is and what it does to you. By beginning to see the false self in this way, you will be awakening the *true self* within. The true self is that within us which sees the false self for what it is and is attuned to the energies of the Spirit of God. To empower the true self to understand the nature of the false self; we are already moving deeper into a conversion process, or spiritual awakening.

In our growth in Christian spirituality, then, we want to come closer and closer to the Lord. Recognizing the false self as the obstacle to this closeness, out of our love of the Lord, we become intent on naming it and letting it go. Every time we let go of a little bit of the false self system, we experience greater detachment, freedom, and serenity.

Characteristics of the False Self System

Consider the characteristics of the false self system listed below. For each one that applies to you, write on a separate sheet of paper or in your journal how you experience this characteristic in your everyday life and what consequences you and others suffer because of it.

1. I am more in touch with what I want for my life than with what God wants for my life.
2. I frequently feel numb, empty, or cranky inside myself.
3. I am afraid to discover what's really going on deep inside myself, and I try to avoid this by living on a more superficial level.
4. When I become uncomfortable inside myself, I find some way to escape from this discomfort by using television, food, work, a relationship, alcohol, drugs, shopping, gambling, reading material, religious activities, or chatter.
5. I am often critical of myself.
6. I am often critical of others.
7. My mind is often filled with anxious preoccupations about the future and about whether I will be able to get or to keep what I think I need.
8. It is difficult for me to just *be*. I generally feel that I must be *doing something* to justify my life to myself.
9. I am trying to find happiness by getting something I don't have or by getting rid of something I do have but don't want.

10. In relationships with others, I generally feel I have to play a role or wear a mask. If I did not do this, others would probably reject me.

11. Frequently, I do not even know what my true thoughts and feelings are.

12. My self-concept or idea of myself is skewed so that I see myself as inferior to others or I see myself as superior to others.

13. I am constantly comparing myself to others to determine if I am "ahead" of them or "behind" them in some area of life.

14. When people insult or ridicule something or someone I am identified with, I feel personally insulted and I become angry. (For example, when my country is criticized, I become defensive.)

15. The roles I play give me a sense of identity. What I do is who I am. If I could not continue to do it, I would not know who I am.

16. When someone criticizes the way I do something, I feel personally put down. I have a hard time separating what I do from my identity.

17. It seems that all my thoughts, feelings, memories, and desires are related to my self-image—to changing it or to maintaining it.

18. If I could better control the people and external circumstances in my life, I would be happier.

19. I tend to view close friends and family members as "mine." I tend to treat them that way, too.

20. I tend to view God as judgmental. I believe I have to do the right things—usually religious kinds of behavior—to win God's approval. I seldom feel that I am in harmony with God.

21. It is hard for me to see how God is involved in the everyday affairs of my life. Generally, it seems that God has nothing to do with me and my life. God has better things to do.

22. In my prayer, I spend more time asking God to do what I want than praying for the grace to do what God wants.

Inventory of Inordinate Desires and Delusions

Desires: In answering the questions below, consider physical health, relationships, present occupation, material comforts, emotional health, sense of God's presence—anything!

1. To want what I do not have! What is this for me?

   a.

   b.

   c.

   d.

   e.

2. There are conditions and circumstances in my life that I am rejecting: I have what I do not want! What are these conditions and circumstances?

   a.

   b.

   c.

   d.

   e.

Delusions

1. On a thinking level, how do my desires reinforce the attitude "I'll be okay when..."?

2. Which of the following are true for you?
I'll be okay when...
a. other people like me.
b. I have good physical health.
c. I retire.
d. I have more money.
e. I have more time to myself.
f. the bishop (my spouse/my boss/my child) does what he/she is supposed to do.
g. (your own personal statements)

Addictive Behaviors Checklist

For each of the characteristics below, check the behaviors that apply to you.

1. When I am feeling down, I frequently turn to this activity to feel better.

2. I am uncomfortable with the way I indulge myself in this behavior.

3. I sometimes lie about my involvement in this behavior.

4. When I go without this activity for a while, I feel uncomfortable and panicky.

5. My behavior in this area causes problems for me (physical, relational, and so on).

6. My behavior in this area causes problems for others.

7. I have tried to stop this behavior, but I inevitably go back to it.

8. When others confront me about this behavior, I become defensive.

9. Because of this behavior, I have cut back on healthy involvements.

10. If I could better control myself in this area, my life would be more manageable.

TOTAL _____

Addictive Behaviors

Alcohol/Drug Intake	Working
Overeating/Undereating	Gambling
Approval-seeking	Religious Activities
Caretaking Others	Watching Television
Sexual Expression	Shopping

If you have one check in any area, it could indicate an addictive involvement. The more checks for any behavior, the more intense the addictive involvement.

Taken from *Freedom from Codependency: A Christian Response* by Philip St. Romain (Liguori Publications, Liguori, Missouri, 1991).

Changing Your Behavior

1. What addiction or false self behavior have you identified that you would like to change? Choose only one to begin, then take another later.
2. Why would you like to change this behavior? What will happen if you do not change it?
3. What need or needs have you been trying to meet or cover up by using this behavior?
4. What are some other ways to meet these needs or to face the problems you are avoiding?

PART THREE

. . . .

Centering
Your Heart
in God's Care

In Part Two, we noted that God is the center of the true self. This is not to say that the true self is God—only that our true self cannot be known until our lives are centered in God. The discovery of God, then, enables the discovery of the true self, and the discovery of the true self reveals our centeredness in God. How, then, do you center your life in God?

First, you must see what kinds of false centers you have been living out of and how this has affected you and others. This was the concern of Part Two. You may, of course, begin to work toward centering your life in God before you have thoroughly unmasked the false self, but it is doubtful that you will get very far until you have done some of this work. If you avoid facing your false self, it will talk you out of the spiritual journey as soon as you get tired. In fact, *the false self is "that" within us which would have us not center our lives in God*. Noticing how this works is a good way to see how the false self operates.

Next, you must ask yourself, "Who is this God, and what would it mean to be centered in God?" These questions put you in touch with your images of God and your ideas about what it means to be a Christian. They address the intellectual dimension of your faith response, and this is very important. Without intellectual conviction, the will has no focus or direction.

Finally, you must decide if you will make God the most important person in your life. If your answer to this is yes, then you will discover that prayer is no longer an option for you but a way of nourishing the deepest hungers of your heart.

Discovering Your Images of God

Listed below are a few suggestions for discovering how your images of God affect your willingness to center your life in God.

1. What words and/or symbols describe how you understood God when you were a young child? How did these affect your willingness to be close to God?

After responding to these questions about your childhood, consider your adolescent years, young adult years, and other times in life up to your present situation.

2. The New Testament teaches us that Jesus Christ is the visible manifestation of the invisible God. (See Colossians 1:15.) In other words, Jesus Christ is the true image of God. If you want to know what God is like, look to Jesus. If you do not know much about Jesus, read the gospels and make notes on what he suggests to you about the true nature of God (especially in his parables).

a. What does Jesus reveal to you about the nature of God?
b. What does Jesus reveal to you about God's attitude toward human beings?
c. How are Jesus' revelations about God like or unlike your own images of God discovered in question one above?

3. Ask your spiritual director or a mature Christian to recommend books that can help you grow to a healthy understanding of God.

Belonging to God

In baptism, you have been claimed by the Church for Christ. Your soul has been grafted into his Mystical Body and so shares in the Life of the Body. But the false self system is capable of rejecting his Life. In Christian spirituality, we strive to live out the meaning of our baptism through a life of faith and love. The following reflections can help you grow in this faith.

1. In a very real sense, your life is most influenced by what you think is most important. What you think most important, you belong to.

a. What or who has been most important in your life through the years?
b. How has this affected your sense of who you are?

2. Christ wants you to belong to him above all. (See Matthew 12:46-50; 13:44-46; 16:24-25; 10:34-39; Luke 18:18-25, and many others.)

    a. To what extent do you experience yourself as belonging to Christ?

    b. How do you feel about belonging to Christ above all else?

    c. What are some of your fears about belonging to Christ?

    d. What attracts you to a commitment of belonging to Christ?

3. To belong to Christ means to entrust your life to his care. This entrusting is what is meant by *faith.*

    a. How have your erroneous images of God affected your willingness to entrust your life to God's care?

    b. Is Jesus Christ a person whom you think you can trust? Why? (Why not?)

    c. Are you willing to entrust your life to the care of Christ? This is the decision of faith.

Walking With Christ

What would it mean to entrust your life to the care of Jesus Christ? Do you just sit back and let him do everything for you? Is there still something you must do? This exercise focuses on these questions by reflecting on the gospel image of being yoked with Jesus.

> *"Come to me, all you who labor and are burdened, and I will give you rest. Take my yoke upon you and learn from me, for I am meek and humble of heart; and you will find*

rest for yourselves. For my yoke is easy, and my burden light" (Matthew 11:28-30).

Implications of the Yoke Image
- Two pulling together, Christ and you. If you do not walk, the yoke will not go forward.
- If you walk too fast or in the wrong direction, Christ will resist this.

1. What are the signs that you are living too fast or too slowly?
2. How do you know when your life is going in the wrong direction?
3. Christ provides the gifts of direction and pace. How do you experience Christ doing this in your life?

Saint Ignatius wrote: "Pray as if everything depends on God, and work as if everything depends on you." Father Anthony de Mello wrote that "God cannot be bothered to do for you what you must do for yourself." The yoke image tells you that you must walk—that Christ cannot walk for you, only *with* you.

1. What are some ways in which you and other people try to get God to do for you what you must do for yourself?
2. What can God do in you and for you that you cannot do for yourself?

A Prayerful Celebration of Entrusting and Commitment

This is a short, powerful way to entrust your life to God's care. Use it frequently.

Prayer

God, I abandon myself into your hands;
  do with me what you will.
 Whatever you may do, I thank you:
 I am ready for all; I accept all
  and in all your creatures—
  I wish no more than this O God.
 Into your hands I commend my soul;
  I offer it to you with all my heart,
  for I love you, God,
  and so need to give myself,
  to surrender myself into your hands without reserve,
   and with boundless confidence,
    for you are my God.

         Charles de Foucauld

Affirmation

God can and will do in me and for me what I could never do for myself.

Commitment

I, for my part, must be willing to use my own human powers in the service of honesty, love, peace. Toward these ends, I am willing

- to claim my will to live because I exist; I will not indulge depressing, life-negating thoughts or feelings
- to love myself because I am alive—because God wills my existence
- to discover and cherish my giftedness, even if others disapprove of my doing so
- to learn healthy, loving ways to meet my needs
- to trust in the loving providence of God concerning the future

- to pray for God's help and to call another person when I feel like indulging my addictive fix
- to keep my attention focused in love all through the day

Prayer

The LORD is my light and my salvation;
    whom do I fear?
The LORD is my life's refuge;
    of whom am I afraid?

....

Though an army encamp against me;
    my heart does not fear.
Though war be waged against me,
    even then do I trust.
One thing I ask of the LORD;
    this I seek:
To dwell in the LORD's house
    all the days of my life,
To gaze on the LORD's beauty,
    to visit his temple.

Psalm 27:1, 3-4

The Holy Spirit

The Holy Spirit is the third Person of the Trinity, who is also one with the Father and the Son. The gift of the Holy Spirit enabled the apostles to move from sorrow and grief to courage and joy. Without the Holy Spirit, we are left to ourselves, trying to imitate and follow Jesus but lacking the will and resolve to do so. We need the Holy Spirit to live the Christian life; without the Holy Spirit, it is impossible to remain centered in God.

With the sacraments of baptism and confirmation, a Christian is blessed with the gift of the Holy Spirit. As with any of God's gifts, however, the Spirit can be neglected to such an extent that we do not even notice the effects in our lives.

To open to the gift of the Holy Spirit, you need only ask. (See Luke 11:13.) When you ask for the gift of the Spirit to enable you to know God's will and to act accordingly, you may be sure that your prayer is answered.

The presence of the Holy Spirit is experienced in many ways:

- as a firm inner resolve to live for Christ
- as a gentle guidance in your thinking process
- as an inner Presence of sweetness, peace, and joy
- as a firm inner opposition to wrongdoing
- as the Source of your desire to pray—especially in praise

Pray often to the Holy Spirit! You need not use a special prayer, although many such prayers exist. Ask in your own words for the Spirit to manifest as described above. Ask throughout the day, and learn to live in the guidance of the Spirit.

The Eucharist

The Christian plan is for the sick and weakened human soul to be joined with the divine/human person of Christ and so to be strengthened to live as God has intended for us to live. We are not saved by "doing the right things" or through spiritual disciplines but by virtue of our union with the living and risen Christ.

Union with Christ begins with baptism and deepens through living a life of faith, hope, and love. Our union with him is a gift, not something we earn; on our own, there is absolutely nothing we can do to attain union with him. That we meet him in prayer and through faith are due to his generosity, not to our deservingness.

When Jesus ascended to the right hand of the Father, he did not go away: he disappeared! This means that he no longer manifested in a localized, physical human form to only a small group but became present to the whole universe through the realm of the Spirit. It is through this realm that he continues to come to us, especially through the gift of the Eucharist.

At every Mass, Christ is manifest in and through the gathered assembly, the Scriptures, the priest, and the consecrated bread and wine. We need to allow ourselves to be nourished in all these ways.

In receiving the consecrated bread and wine, we receive the body and blood of Christ and are joined in the word most intimately with our priest and our community to his invisible, living Body of Christ. When we eat regular food, it becomes part of our human body; when we consume the body and blood of Christ, we become part of his Body.

The gift of the Eucharist is Christ feeding his Church. We need this food, and we need it often. The Church recommends that all Catholics be nourished by Eucharist at least once a week. This is a minimal requirement. More frequent participation in Mass and reception of the Eucharist is strongly encouraged if we wish to grow closer to Christ.

Basics of Personal Prayer

Just as two lovers cannot grow closer without taking special time to talk to each other and be together, so it is with you and Christ. This is why personal prayer is so important. As Saint

Alphonsus so beautifully put it, "Prayer is talking and listening to God about the things that pertain to our friendship."

Prayer is so obviously necessary for growth in Christ. Why are so few Christians really committed to spending time with God daily? The answer again is the false self system. Prayer spells death to the false self, and the false self exists to control our lives according to its own fearful values. Prayer, on the other hand, invites *God* to direct our lives. You can see how the false self would perceive this as a conflict.

All the excuses people use to avoid daily prayer come from the false self, and not one of them has any real validity! It may be, for example, that there are mornings when we don't have time because the alarm clock fails to ring or a small child's needs take precedence. But these are exceptional situations. Everyone has plenty of time for prayer. If nothing else, we can get up earlier to pray; sleep lost for prayer will not be missed.

A first consideration for growing in prayer, then, is that you must make a *commitment of time* to be with God daily. I recommend a minimum of twenty to thirty minutes. It takes that long just to quiet down and listen. If possible, choose a time of the day when you are awake and energetic. (Bringing to God your leftover psychic energy at the end of the day might be the best you can do, but how would you like it if your lover did this to you every time?) Getting started is the hard part, and the false self will put up a great resistance. After a few weeks, though, you will wonder how you ever lived without prayer. (If you are already taking this time, you know very well what I mean.)

Personal prayer time is to be spent in a context of *silence* and *solitude*. Communal prayer is very good, but it is no substitute for one-on-one time with God. You would not talk to your lover only in a crowd, would you? So, too, with God. Find a place where you can be alone and undisturbed. Ask your family to leave you in peace during your prayer time; they will benefit from the more peaceful and joyful attitude you bring

to them. Ask them to take a message if you receive a phone call.

How do you spend this time with God? You may do whatever you wish, of course, and God will bless you for it. But to really enter into a sharing or dialogue with God, a simple format such as that described below works very well for most people.

1. *Quieting.* Take a few moments to come into the present. Notice the sounds around you, the feel of your clothing, your breathing. Ask the Holy Spirit to guide you in this time.

2. *Listening.* Read a short passage of Scripture slowly. Sometimes reading it aloud helps bring it to life. The passage you select should be something that provides food for thought. (You wouldn't want a genealogy, for example.) New Testament passages are most recommended—especially the gospel readings used by the Church for daily Mass. After reading the passage once, read it again, even more slowly, letting the message sink in. Here is a message to you from God.

3. *Meditation.* In Christianity, meditation means using your mind to consider the meaning of a sacred reading. If the reading touches off a spontaneous meditation, stay with it. This might mean sharing with God what you think and feel about what you have read. You might also want to use your imagination to meditate. For example, try to see Jesus standing before you, speaking the words of Scripture. Some meditation books are also helpful for breaking open the Word of God. (See Suggested Reading, page 111.)

4. *Affective Prayer.* After listening to the Word and considering its meaning to you, pray for the grace to carry out its message this day. You might be moved to pray for others, to thank God for favors received, or to express sorrow for shortcomings. This kind of prayer may come before listening and meditating if you are experiencing many feelings and preoccupations.

Lift them up to the Lord first, and then you will have a quiet place within to listen.

5. *Silent Adoration.* It is good to just "be" with God in silence and love. Sometimes this will be easy for you—a natural and spontaneous outgrowth of your dialogue with God. Regardless, simply be silent before God during the final five to ten minutes of prayer. If you begin to practice centering prayer (see Appendix One on page 85), you may wish to be silent even longer. You might envision God as an invisible, loving Light and feel yourself being silently energized by this Light. You might also use a simple word or short phrase ("Praise you, Lord God" or "My Lord and my God") to bring your attention to God in silence.

As the months and years go by, you will find yourself becoming drawn more and more to silent forms of prayer. This resting in God in loving silence is called *contemplative prayer.* Even advanced contemplatives, however, recommend beginning with a short period of listening and meditating before letting themselves plunge into the deep Silence. Listening and meditating prepare the mind for this Silence and enable you to rest there in peace and stability.

Spiritual Direction

It is helpful to have a companion with whom you can share your joys and struggles in living the Christian life. This companion may be your spouse, another family member, or a close friend.

When we speak of spiritual direction, however, we are referring to a relationship that is more specifically focused on helping you live in faith. A spiritual director listens and gives feedback about what he or she is hearing and sensing about the movement of the Holy Spirit in your life. This feedback is for your consideration only; the spiritual director is not a guru who tells you what to do.

The ideal of spiritual direction is soundly rooted in our understanding of Christian community. The Christian journey is not meant to be an individualistic, privatized spirituality. It is in community that we discover who we are and what we have to share. Spiritual direction provides an opportunity for a friendly and discerning experience of Christian community. As a community of two, you and the spiritual director attempt to discern what the Spirit is doing in your life and how you are being called to share your giftedness.

Spiritual Direction and Psychotherapy: From the foregoing, it should already be obvious that spiritual direction is fundamentally different from psychotherapy. A counselor is not concerned with your spiritual center nor with how the Holy Spirit is leading you. The goals of psychotherapy are different: they are usually to help you deal with painful emotions and to support you in making difficult choices about relationships.

A spiritual director may deal with the same issues but from a quite different perspective. Painful feelings may be discussed in terms of how they lead away from God or toward God. Difficult relationships are also reviewed to discern how God is calling us to love other people and ourselves as well.

Because spiritual direction and psychotherapy have different goals and emphases, it is possible to benefit from both at the same time. A person who is in counseling should not refrain from spiritual direction because of it. Nor should anyone choose a spiritual director over a counselor. In fact, spiritual directors who guide people away from psychotherapy are doing their directees a disservice.

It sometimes happens that a spiritual director is also a trained counselor. Even so, the director and directee need to be clear about precisely what is going on in their work together.

Finally, we note that psychotherapists generally meet with their clients once a week or more. Such frequent meetings are necessary to process the many feelings and attitudinal changes going on in the person's life. Spiritual directors, on the other hand, seldom meet with directees more than once every two weeks in the beginning of the relationship. After a while, once a month is usually sufficient.

The Agenda in Spiritual Direction: Some spiritual directors have a set agenda for time spent with their directees; most do not. You will usually be allowed to talk about anything you have on your mind. If your sharing seems to have nothing to do with living the Christian life, the director will eventually try to steer the discussion in that direction by asking how what you have shared is affecting your prayer life or your relationship with God.

Usually, the first few meetings will be spent just getting to know each other. The director will want to know all about your life. Telling your story to another in this way will help you come to know yourself better; the listening presence of the director is also a source of great healing. Because the spiritual director is not in the same role as a counselor, he or she may also choose to tell you much about his or her life and faith journey. This can help you see the director as a fellow pilgrim on the journey rather than as a guru with all the answers.

After getting to know each other, you and the director may decide on a few structured activities to work on (such as those in this book), or you may agree to go through a book on spiritual growth together. Many directors are trained in the Spiritual Exercises of Saint Ignatius and use these in some manner with their directees. I like to use the Twelve Steps with people I work with. Some directors with special training may also invite you to together. Others know a great deal about keeping a personal journal and may encourage you to keep one if you haven't already started doing so. Most directors these days also respect the fact that different human temperaments are drawn in different ways by the Spirit, so they might want to help you discover your personality type.

As you can see, many kinds of issues can be discussed in spiritual direction. Of paramount importance, however, is your life of prayer. A spiritual director is one who will hold you accountable for daily prayer. He or she will be interested in hearing what is happening during your prayer and will help you deepen your growth in prayer.

Choosing a Spiritual Director: We have already noted that a spiritual director is not a guru who will tell you what to do and what not to do. I would also like to make a distinction between a spiritual director and a sponsor in a Twelve Step program. A sponsor is one who has been in such a program for some time and can help new people learn how to recover from addictive involvements by using the Twelve Steps. This is a form of spiritual companionship, to be sure, but I recommend that your spiritual director be more than just a "big buddy" for the spiritual journey.

Ideally, your spiritual director should be a person with some formal training or experience in this area. He or she should have knowledge of the Catholic mystical tradition and should be at least generally familiar with psychological development. Your director should be a person of prayer who has attended one or more eight-day silent directed retreats. Finally, he or she should also be in spiritual direction with another and should have already worked through painful issues from the past.

I consider these minimal requirements for a Catholic spiritual director. Not many meet these requirements, but there are enough who do. Generally, the ministry staff at a retreat center are good resources for finding a spiritual director. Most religious communities also have a few qualified people. Diocesan priests can be found who meet the minimal requirements, and more laypeople than ever are functioning effectively in this role.

If you do not already have a spiritual director and don't know whom to ask, I suggest you call your local retreat house. If you know of no such center, ask your parish priest for advice. Even after choosing someone, do not think you have to stay with that person. Agree with your director to give the relationship a trial for a while. Then, after a few sessions, evaluate whether you feel comfortable enough to continue.

Fees: It is typical for Christians to view ministry as something they have already paid for in the Sunday collection. This holds true for many parish services, but that is the limit.

Spiritual direction is really a professional service; therefore, be prepared to offer compensation to your director—especially if he or she is not an employee of the parish to which you tithe. Typically, the director will suggest that you make a donation to his or her retreat center or religious community. Some directors are self-employed; in this case, your compensation would be given directly to the individual.

Seldom does a director have a set fee such as psychotherapists do, and you would probably never be refused for nonpayment. Nevertheless, I recommend a minimum donation of fifteen dollars per session. If this is more than you can afford, give what you can—even if it is a batch of cookies or a handwritten thank-you note. You will feel better for giving something in return for this service, and your director will appreciate it, too.

PART
FOUR

· ·

Reconciliation
and Inner
Transformation

It has been said that the love of God is "obtained" through faith, prayer, and sacrament but "retained" through the love of neighbor. Another saying has it that "you can't give what you don't have, but you can't keep what you don't share." These are very important spiritual principles.

Part Three was concerned with cultivating a personal relationship with God through Christ. This is very much according to the will of Christ, who said, "Come to me, all you who labor and are burdened, and I will give you rest" (Matthew 11: 28). Jesus wants us to share in his own special love-bond (the Holy

Spirit) with the Father and to grow in that love. This is the new life that will go on forever.

Spiritual growth, as already mentioned, is not to be a private matter. We cannot grow in the love of God without growing in the love of ourselves and other people. "If anyone says, 'I love God,' but hates his brother, he is a liar" (1 John 4:20). Indeed, it seems that the love of God that comes through faith, prayer, and sacrament is directly related to our love of neighbor. In the Lord's Prayer we learn that God will forgive us our trespasses as we forgive others. In another place, we hear Jesus saying that reconciliation with our neighbor is a prerequisite for authentic prayer and worship. (See Matthew 5:23-24.) God will not allow us to use his love as a drug with which to escape our responsibility to build a healthy human community.

Part Four will present resources to help you examine your human relationships, to make amends where necessary, and to forgive those who have wronged you. Not only are these things important for ongoing spiritual growth, the false self feeds upon the guilt, fear, shame, resentment, and hurt resulting from troubled relationships. These painful emotional energies pull you away from your true center and influence you to adopt a defensive, controlling posture toward others. If you are to grow spiritually, you will need to diminish the power of the false self in your consciousness, and one of the best ways to do this is to starve it to death by depriving it of emotional pain. Forgiveness and reconciliation are the ways to obtain this healing.

Renewal of Mind

In addition to the healing of emotions, a healing of attitudes is also called for. Reconciling with others will do you no good if you persist in old habits of judging, criticizing, and blaming yourself and others for things that are relatively unimportant. To grow spiritually, you must "be transformed by the renewal of your mind, that you may discern what is the will of God, what is good and pleasing and perfect" (Romans 12:2). In addition, "you should put away the old self of your former way of life, corrupted through deceitful desires, and be renewed in the spirit of your minds, and put on the new self, created in God's way in righteousness and holiness of truth" (Ephesians 4:22-24). If you do not change your habits of thinking and judging, the false self system will continue to create misery for you and project ill-will in all your relationships.

Many unhealthy attitudes are changed through prayer and meditation. Even so, ongoing vigilance is necessary. You must learn to detect negative and judgmental thoughts as soon as they begin and redirect your thinking in a more rational and loving direction. This is unquestionably the most difficult work of all in the process of spiritual transformation. Old, negative habits of thinking and judging can be so deeply ingrained that they function automatically and reactively without your permission—even against your will. "For I do not do the good I want, but I do the evil I do not want. Now if [I] do what I do not want, it is no longer I who do it, but sin that dwells in me" (Romans 7:19-20).

Through your ongoing efforts to live a spiritual life, you come to recognize in yourself another will or energy that stands in opposition to the automatic, judgmental reactions of the false self. The encounter between this spiritual will and the false self system is nothing short of an inner civil war. Many people turn back when this war begins. As noted earlier, it is a most difficult time on the journey. But to turn back is only to guarantee victory for the false self system. There is nothing to do but to live through the civil war, knowing that its turbulent commotion is a very good sign that inner transformation is taking place.

In the meantime, you can do a few things to help yourself.

1. You can continue to be faithful through prayer, Eucharist, and reconciliation with others.
2. You can rejoice that this civil war is taking place within you, rather than running away from it. In time the war will end, for the victory has already been won by Christ.
3. Inner transformation is a time when spiritual direction is also very helpful; you need this support to carry on.
4. Finally, you can practice affirmations that help to implant deep within you a healthier system of thoughts and judgments. A few suggestions toward this end are provided in this section.

Examen of Current Relationships

Name the person with whom you are in relationship.

1. What do you and this person do together or have in common?

2. How would you describe the bond that exists between you?
   • Intellectually • Emotionally • Spiritually

3. Affirmations:
   • What qualities of character do you admire in this person?

- Which of this person's behaviors do you most appreciate? (Resolve to tell him or her about this at some time.)

4. Difficulties:
- Which of this person's behaviors are hard for you to accept? How do you feel about each of these behaviors?

5. What could *you* do more of and less of to improve this relationship? Be very specific in terms of behavior—something you can *do*.

More of   **Less of**

6. What would you like the *other person* to *do* more of and less of to help improve this relationship? (Resolve to ask for these changes at some time in the future.)

More of   **Less of**

Preparing for Reconciliation With Others

Reconciling with other people requires preparation, and I can think of no better approach than Step Eight of the Twelve Steps: *Made a list of all persons we had harmed and became willing to make amends to them all.*

There are three key concepts in this statement.

1. *Made a list.* It is important to evaluate a relationship carefully before attempting some kind of reconciliation with the other.
2. *All persons we had harmed.* We first need to see how our lives have affected others. After doing so, we may see how others have hurt us in some manner.
3. *Willing to make amends to them all.* This quality of willingness is absolutely necessary. Without it, we will not be able to release our hurts and resentments.

Examining Your Relationships: To prepare yourself for reconciliation with others, I suggest you review your relationship with one person at a time, responding to the following questions:

1. What has a relationship with this person meant to me during the different times of my life?
2. What specific situations have contributed to problems between us?
3. How have I hurt this person by word, deed, or neglect?
   - How do I feel about each of these?
   - What have been the consequences to this person, to me, and to our relationship?
4. How has this person hurt or angered me by words, deeds, or neglect?

- How do I feel about each of these?
- What have been the consequences to this person, to me, and to our relationship?

These are obviously very difficult questions to answer. If you have never reviewed your relationships before, I suggest that you take at least one good, hard look at them using this format. After going through this reflection and following through in the manner suggested in the next exercise, you will be more free from painful emotions related to relationships. This freedom will enable you to maintain yourself in a stance of centeredness in Christ.

You may find it helpful to share your reflections from this exercise with your spiritual director before planning to take any action. It helps to share these hurts with another, and your spiritual director will accept you and listen to you no matter what you have discovered about yourself. This can increase both your willingness to make amends and your readiness to do so.

Reconciling With Others

This exercise is a follow-up to the previous one, "Preparing for Reconciliation With Others." It is based on Step Nine of the Twelve Steps: *Made direct amends to such people whenever possible, except when to do so would injure them or others.*

Having honestly evaluated your relationships in the spirit of the eighth step, you must now decide what to do about these relationships. Holding on to old hurts and resentments hurts you much more than it hurts another, and yet the ninth step points out the importance of using discretion in attempting reconciliation.

As in the previous exercise, we make a distinction here between what you have done to others and what they have done to you. In reconciling with others, you must make amends for the harm you have done to them, and you must forgive them for the hurts they have caused you. Making amends and forgiving others are the two methods of reconciling with others. I suggest you consider them separately, although they are surely related.

For each relationship you examined in the previous exercise, consider now the following questions:

1. What kinds of amends must I make?

- *Apologies for specific behaviors.* Mention consequences: "I apologize for cursing at you when we argued last week. I know this hurt your feelings and that you felt embarrassed when your friends laughed about my remark. I've felt badly about this ever since."

This kind of sharing may be done in direct personal communication, by phone, or in writing.

- *Making restitution.* Repaying money or repairing damages done. Returning something gained from dishonest behavior. This, too, may be done in writing or through verbal communication.
- *Doing nothing.* If making amends will hurt the other person unnecessarily, it is better to do nothing. Your amends can be your ongoing efforts to be honest and loving.

2. How can I forgive this person?

- *Communicate directly.* Tell the other person what he or she did or said that hurt or angered you. Discuss the behavior and how you felt; do not discuss motives, which you do not know. Finally, let the other person know that you forgive him or her. You may also ask for a change of behavior. For example, you might say, "Last week when you came home late without calling, I felt hurt and very angry that you didn't even acknowledge it when you finally did arrive. I have decided to forgive you for this—I will not mention it again, and I will let go of my anger about it—but I do ask that you call me the next time you will be late." (*Note:* This kind of communication works best if shared person to person, but it may be better to write it to the other if you have trouble sharing feelings verbally.)

- *Write a letter.* But do not mail it or share it with the other person. (You may choose to share it with your spiritual director, however.) This is often the best approach in relationships where the other person is still too unhealthy to listen to you without harming you. It also works well in relationships with persons who have died. In the latter case, you may choose to read your letter at the grave site or in another, prayerful context.

Letting Go of the Past: After making your best efforts to forgive others and to make amends, you have done all that spirituality asks you to do to be at peace with your past. Let the past be. It is normal for emotions about the past to remain for some time after reconciliation, so you need not see this as a sign that you haven't forgiven (unless something new and important is presenting itself through your memory, that is). Let the past be. Do not meddle in it any longer. In time, painful emotions about the past will fade.

A special word must be said about situations where people discover that they have been severely abused in the past. Forgiveness may not come easily in this case, and emotions may be very turbulent. Do not hesitate to seek professional counseling to deal with these issues. Eventually, you must forgive those who have abused you to be free within yourself, but it may take the support of both spiritual direction and psychotherapy for you to do so.

Daily Examen

Many of the exercises presented in this book invite you to take a long, hard look at your life. This is especially important if you have never done so. But such comprehensive self-examination and reflection is not the norm for those living a spiritual life. They are major housecleanings, as it were. Once the house is clean, you do not clean it all over again (unless you are compulsive about such matters); you try to keep it clean, which takes a little effort each day. Such a small daily inner housecleaning is the *examen.*

Daily examen is usually done at the end of the day to look back on the day and learn whatever lessons suggest themselves. I recommend at least fifteen minutes for this, which can be taken as a form of prayerful meditation or even a prayerful walk before bedtime. The format below describes some of the issues the examen ought to consider:

1. Begin with prayer to the Holy Spirit for guidance in looking back on your day.
2. If there is a strong feeling or issue on your mind, acknowledge this and note its relevance to living a spiritual life. What is the Lord inviting you to do about this issue?
3. If there is no strong feeling—or after dealing with such an issue—slowly and prayerfully recall the events of your day as you experienced them. You need not dwell on any particular part of the day unless you discover strong or hidden feelings you had not noticed before, in which case

you return to the approach suggested in the second point for dealing with such matters.

4. Having examined the events of your day, what have you earned?
   - When did you feel close to God?
   - When did you pull away from God? Ask for pardon.
   - What kind of growth do you note?
   - Do you need to forgive anyone or to make amends? If so, resolve to do so as soon as possible.

5. Thank God for this day, and pray for a peaceful sleep.

Regular practice of the examen will help you to sleep well, for your mind will have come to rest before you go to bed. Consequently, your dreams will be more peaceful, and you will wake up feeling refreshed.

The examen will also help you to grow in self-knowledge and will enable you to discover how you are living your spirituality each day. Using a journal for your examen can help you keep track of progress through the days and weeks as well as identify issues for discussion with your spiritual director or in the sacrament of reconciliation (penance).

As with many other things, the examen is a discipline. Along with prayer and frequent reception of the Eucharist, I consider the examen to be an indispensable tool for spiritual growth. If you practice it faithfully for a month, you will surely discover for yourself what I am talking about, and the discipline will become one that you look forward to.

The Sacrament of Reconciliation

To help Christians live a spiritual life, the Catholic Church makes available the sacrament of reconciliation (also called the sacrament of penance). We recognize that there are times when our behavior proceeds from the false self, and this hurts other people and ourselves as well. When this happens, we must work toward reconciliation in our relationships.

But there is another dimension to this sinful behavior. Acting out of the false self means that we have broken relationship with God and so lost touch with our True Center. If we are to treat God as the most important Person in our lives, we must be reconciled with God when we stray. This is the opportunity the sacrament of reconciliation extends to us. ·

This is not the place to discuss the proper way to prepare for the sacrament or to explain the rite itself. If you do not know how to do this, you can surely receive information and instruction from your local parish. Your reflections from the previous exercises (especially Steps Eight and Nine and the Daily Examen) can be used as part of your sharing, but other matters should be considered as well—such as how you have been fulfilling your obligations to the Christian community.

The sacrament of reconciliation can help you to honestly renew your commitment to God when you have seriously lost your way. Therefore, it is to be treated as an important resource for living a Christian spiritual life.

Inner Transformation and Healing

A Guided Meditation or Journaling Exercise

First find a comfortable position, take several deep breaths, and relax.

1. Pay attention to the kinds of thoughts, feelings, and images going on in your consciousness.

2. Identify preoccupations that seem to convey the theme "I'll be okay when..." Label all of these as specifically as possible. For example, "I'll be okay when I lose twenty pounds."

3. Restate the preoccupation in a negative sense. For example, "I'm not okay because I'm twenty pounds overweight."

4. How do you feel about this "not being okay because..."? For example, "Because I'm overweight, I feel ashamed and embarrassed."

5. What are specific circumstances when you have felt this way? For example, "I feel ashamed and embarrassed about my weight when I go to family get-togethers or parties." Allow yourself to feel these feelings.

6. What do you need from God, from yourself, or from other people when you feel this way? For example, "When I feel ashamed and 'fat,' I need to know that I am still loved and valued as a person."

7. Invite the Holy Spirit to speak to you and console you in your feelings of pain. Pray for the grace to be healed from these painful emotions. (See Romans 8:35-39, John 14:27-31, Matthew 11:28-30.)

8. Allow yourself to feel loved even in your pain.

9. As self-affirmation, speak from your conscious rational self a nurturing phrase to your emotional experience. For example, "I'm a lovable person." Address your inner child with an affirmation such as "You are loved by me, no matter what."

10. See yourself in a circumstance usually difficult for you; feel yourself as a loving, lovable person in this circumstance. Repeat your affirmation, if necessary. This is called *positive imaging.*

Affirmations
for a Loving Attitude

A*ffirmations* are sentences used to improve one's attitude and to focus more clearly in a positive manner. It is best to speak affirmations with the lips (even quietly so, as in a whisper) rather than simply to repeat them mentally. They may also be used with the imagination, to envision yourself speaking these words to another person or to hear God speaking these words to you.

As you meditate with affirmations, you may discover that feelings come up that tend to support the affirmation being expressed. Allow this to happen, for it will help you carry forward your resolve. You may also discover attitudes and feelings that seem to go against the direction of the affirmation. Observe this and feel it, but don't get involved in willfully trying to reverse these sentiments. Simply persevere in your meditation with affirmations, and in time these old emotional attitudes will be reversed.

God Affirming You: In prayer, imagine God standing before you, speaking.
- *I am here for you, no matter where you may be.*
- *I am here with you, no matter what you may feel.*
- *You are always acceptable to me, no matter what other people (or you) may think about you.*
- *I see and appreciate the many good things you do each day.*
- *I see and appreciate your good intentions, even when you fail to carry them out with your behavior.*
- *I see your ill-intentions and behavior, but I love you all the same and forgive you everything even before you ask.*

- *I see your stubbornness and unwillingness to change, but I will wait forever if that's how long it takes for you to respond to my love.*
- *I am here to serve you unto happiness.*

Affirmations Expressing Love for Another Person: Envision this person in some manner, and speak these words to the person with your mind.

- *I wish you peace, joy, and well-being.*
- *You are always acceptable to me, regardless of your behavior.*
- *I am here to serve you unto happiness, in whatever way is appropriate.*
- *I see and appreciate the many good things you do each day.*
- *I do not know your heart or intentions, so I do not judge you, even when your behavior is out of line.*
- *I forgive you every wrong you have done me, and I ask that you forgive me as well.*
- *Even if you do not return my love, I will still love you and hope in you.*

Affirmations for Healthy Boundaries in Relationships: Envision a person and speak these words to this person in your mind.

- *I decide what I am willing to do or not do for you and another.*
- *I have a right to say no to you when my needs take precedence.*
- *I have a right to ask for anything I want in a relationship, but I leave you free to respond.*

- *I allow you to make your own decisions.* (Note: *parents must be involved in helping their children make decisions.*)
- *I allow you to make mistakes and suffer the consequences.*
- *I am willing to confront behavior that bothers me and to take measures to protect myself from unnecessary hurt.*

Affirmations and Self-Image

Read these affirmations slowly and prayerfully in solitude and silence. You may also write them in your journal just before sleep for a deeper impact. Spend at least twenty minutes with them each day until your negative self-talk becomes minimal.

1. If God is for me, who can be against me?
2. I am lovable and acceptable because I exist—because God is choosing to love me into existence in this now-moment, and "God doesn't make junk."
3. I know how to do many things that can contribute to the improvement of the human community. If I do not share my giftedness, it will be missed by others.
4. I do not judge myself as a bad person when I make mistakes or deviate from a social norm.
5. I do not judge myself as a bad person when I hurt another with my behavior. I take responsibility for my behavior and make amends.
6. It is unreasonable for me to expect perfection of myself. I will do the best I can, and that is all that God expects.
7. I accept my physical appearance. If others reject me on this basis, it is not because I am unlovable but because they are

comparing my appearance to a social norm propagated largely by the media.

8. I accept all of my feelings, pleasant and unpleasant, knowing that I am more than my feelings. Feelings come and go. They do not reveal to me my true worth as a person. I do not define myself on the basis of my feelings but on my faith-convictions.

9. Other people have judged me and mistreated me, and this has affected my view of myself. I am more than what others have told me I am, so I do not accept their judgments of me.

10. I forgive everyone everything they have done that has hurt me, for I know that holding on to hurt and resentment will keep me from growing to be the person God created me to be.

11. I take responsibility for meeting my own needs in a moral and loving manner. It is not someone else's responsibility to meet my needs.

12. I am in doubt about my beauty and worth. I ask God to help me to see and know myself as God sees and knows me.

13. Right now, I am where I should be in life. I have learned many lessons and have many more to learn. That is life: learning and growing. It is good for me to be here in life.

14. Right now, I have everything I need to be as happy as it is possible for me to be in this life. Therefore, I renounce the idea that my present circumstances are inadequate for happiness, that I need more of something or another, or that I need less of something or another. Happiness is an attitude, not an acquisition. In gratitude to God, I accept myself and my life just as they are.

PART FIVE

. . . .

Living in the Spirit

Up to this point, the exercises in this book have focused on helping you become established in your spiritual center and grow in that life through prayer and healing. They have largely emphasized your inner life in order to help you move from a life centered in people and circumstances outside yourself (the centeredness of the false self) to a life centered in relationship with the Spirit within.

But life cannot be spent looking inward! Through an ongoing life of prayer, with daily examen and frequent reception of the Eucharist, you may trust that growth in your spiritual center will deepen and hold. The primary issues then move from concern about where you are centered to living in the Spirit all through the day.

Living constantly in the Spirit is not as easy as it may sound however. Even those who have been living a spiritual life for years must still struggle with worldly temptations to pursue pleasure, popularity, wealth, and all the other addictions the false self is prone to. You must also learn to meet your needs in a healthy manner. More than likely, you have learned to meet your basic needs in somewhat of a false self mentality. We all have! Now, however, you must learn just what are your real human needs and what are mere wants and desires. This is where the influence of the world can confuse you. So Part Five will attempt to provide some direction in this area.

Discerning God's will is another issue that pertains to daily living. You have many gifts and talents—some of which you are already using in various ways, some of which you may not yet even recognize.

What is God calling you to do with these gifts and talents? A discerning response to this question enables you to remain centered in the Spirit all day long.

Finally, there is the issue of suffering. When the going gets rough, many abandon the spiritual journey. Sometimes it may happen that the pains you experience are directly related to your life in Christ—that if you were living a more worldly life, you wouldn't be experiencing rejection or inner conflict. These times are very important! They are experiences of the cross of Christ. When you reject a cross, you fall back into the domain of the false self. By learning to carry these crosses, you will experience a deepening of the love and fellowship of the Holy Spirit.

Meeting Your True Needs

God has made us to be creatures with a wide variety of needs. In pursuing the fulfillment of these needs, human beings encounter one another and the creation. What is the nature of these encounters? And what kinds of needs are we attentive to? These are moral and spiritual issues no Christian can avoid facing.

As an adult and a Christian, it is your responsibility to meet your own needs. You cannot do this alone, of course, but neither should you expect that other people will take responsibility for knowing your needs and seeing to it that you care for yourself. Perhaps the best way to love yourself is to attend to your needs in healthy and responsible ways. In caring for yourself in this manner, you will be moved into contact with other human beings upon whom you depend for helping you meet your needs. Everyone is doing the same; this is how human community and culture are formed.

But what are your needs? How can you distinguish them from your wants?

These questions are not easy to answer. Generally, a need is considered to be a basic requirement for human health and wholeness; if you do not meet such a need, you are less healthy and whole. Wants are something altogether different and refer to the requirements of the false self. Quite frequently wants are superimposed on our needs, such as when we purchase clothing for the purpose of being in style as well as for covering the body. Indeed, you will likely discover that the wants of the false self have influenced the way you have been meeting your needs all along.

Living in the Spirit does not mean that you cease to have needs, only that you learn to meet them without giving in to the wants of the false self.

For each of the needs listed below, consider the following four questions:

1. How have I met this need in the past?
2. How have the concerns of the false self influenced the way I have met this need?
3. How could this need be met in a healthy and responsible manner, free from the wants of the false self?
4. What, specifically, will I do to meet these needs in my life from now on?

Physical Needs
- Food, water, nutrition
- Exercise
- Sleep
- Shelter
- Clothing
- Medical care when sick

Psychospiritual Needs
- Play/fun/humor
- Honest, caring relationships
- Sense of choice, freedom
- Sense of purpose, meaning, hope
- Intellectual stimulation
- Aesthetic stimulation
- Prayer
- Creative expression

Sharing Your Giftedness

Each individual is unique. God has blessed you with gifts in a way that no one else is blessed. Your special gift may be something as simple as the ability to listen and empathize with others or as public as preaching the Good News. Whatever your gifts, it is certain that your ongoing spiritual growth will depend on your sharing them in some manner for the good of the Church. When you share your gifts, you are blessed; and this blessing brings a love of ministry.

The following questions are designed to help you discover your perception of your giftedness and how you are called to share yourself at this time in your life:

1. What kinds of gifts do I have to offer that may be of service to people?
2. How am I sharing these gifts at this time in my life?
3. Are there other gifts I think I might have?
4. What are some ways to develop my giftedness more fully?

Dreaming: Assume that money is no problem, and you can design your lifestyle any way you choose. Answer the following questions and give your reasons for each.

1. Would you be married, single, in a religious community?
2. If you are not married and would like to be, what qualities do you look for in a spouse? Would you like children to be part of your life?
3. Where would you like to live? What kind of home or living situation do you want?
4. What kind of work would you like to do?
5. How would you spend your time on a typical day?

6. How does answering these questions help you to actualize and express your giftedness?
7. How does the lifestyle you dream of reflect the values of your spiritual center?
8. If you are not already living this lifestyle, what stops you from doing so? What do you want to do about this obstacle to realizing your dreams?

Discerning God's Will

The following suggestions are taken from my book *Pathways to Serenity* (Liguori Publications, 1988) and rely heavily on the guidelines for the discernment of spirits in *The Spiritual Exercises* of Saint Ignatius Loyola. They are to be used when attempting to discern God's will in major decisions about your life.

Theological Assumptions Relevant to Discernment
1. God is a good God. God wants to give you much more than you want for yourself.
2. God knows who you are better than you know yourself. God also knows what you need in order to become the person he created better than you know this about yourself.
3. When you are faced with a number of options, it is entirely possible that some are better for you in terms of your overall human growth than others.
4. When you surrender your preferences for different options to God, you become free to discern God's preference (if any) among these options.

Principles for Spiritual Decision Making
1. "When you are making a decision or choice, you are not deliberating about choices which involve sin (wrongdoing),

but rather you are considering alternatives which are lawful and good..." (Saint Ignatius).

2. It is not necessary to agonize over God's will in choosing between healthy options in the small affairs of everyday life. "Ordinarily there is nothing of such obvious importance in one rather than the other that there is need to go into long deliberation over it. You must proceed in good faith and without making subtle distinctions in such affairs and, as Saint Basil says, do freely what seems good to you so as not to weary your mind, waste your time, and put yourself in danger of disquiet, scruples, and superstitions" (Saint Francis de Sales).

3. In areas where you have binding commitments (such as marriage vows, parenting, religious vows), "your basic attitude should be that the only choice still called for is the full-hearted gift of self to this state of life" (Saint Ignatius). In other words, every effort must be made to live out the implications of your binding commitments, even if those commitments were poorly made. This does not mean that you must suffer unnecessary abuse at the hands of another, however.

4. In areas of life where you have already made decisions that can be changed on the basis of what you had once discerned to be God's will, "your one desire should be to find your continued growth in the way of life you have chosen" (Saint Ignatius).

5. "If you have come to a poor decision in matters that are changeable, you should try to make a choice in the proper way whether it would be maintaining the same pattern of life or it would demand a change" (Saint Ignatius).

6. If possible, you should avoid making important life decisions during times when you are emotionally upset, for it is likely that you would be running away from a problem rather than responding to God's call.

7. When attempting to discern among a number of options

regarding significant lifestyle choices, you would do well to proceed as Saint Ignatius suggests in the following patterns:

First Pattern
- Clearly place before your mind what it is you want to decide about. What are your options?
- Attempt to view each option with equal detachment, surrendering personal preferences to the care of God.
- Sincerely pray that God will enlighten and draw you in the direction leading to his praise and glory.
- List and weigh the advantages and disadvantages of the various dimensions of your proposed decision.
- Consider now which alternative seems more reasonable. Then decide according to the more weighty motives and not from any selfish or sensual inclination.
- Having come to the decision, now turn to God again and ask him to accept and confirm it—if it is for his greater service and glory—by giving you a sense of serenity and holy conviction about this decision.

Second Pattern: This is an excellent follow-up on the First Pattern to evaluate your decision from another angle.

- Since the love of God should motivate your life, check yourself to see whether your attachment to the object of choice is solely because of your Creator and Lord.
- Imagine yourself in the presence of a person whom you have never met before but who has sought your help in an attempt to respond better to God's call. Review what you would tell that person, and then observe the advice you would so readily give to another for whom you want the best.
- Ask yourself if at the moment of death you would make the same decision you are making now. Guide yourself

by this insight, and make your present decision in conformity with it.

- See yourself standing before Christ your Judge when this life has ended and talking with him about the decision you have made at this moment in your life. Choose now the course of action you feel will give you happiness and joy in the presence of Christ on the Day of Judgment.

Guidelines for Healthy Relationships

1. If you cannot love someone, then at least do them no harm.
2. Never do for others what they can and should do for themselves (except as an occasional special surprise).
3. Take time to listen to people. Try to get a feel for what it's like to be in their shoes.
4. Validate the feelings of others by letting them know in a nonjudgmental way that you understand what they're feeling.
5. Take the first step in risking with people. Share something about yourself when appropriate.
6. Empathize with others. Share with them times when you have felt what they're feeling.
7. Learn to affirm people. Let them know that you like them and appreciate them for what they do.
8. Learn to ask for your needs. Let other people know what you would like them to do for you to love you as you would like to be loved.
9. Have fun! Find things to enjoy and laugh about.
10. Always be honest, except when to do so would hurt another.

11. When you need to confront someone, leave personality out of the discussion. Talk about the problem behavior and how it bothers you. Ask for behavior change, and thank the other person if she or he agrees to this. If she or he does not agree to change, decide what you will do to take care of yourself (not to punish the other).

12. When disagreeing with others, make every effort to listen to them to learn the assumptions and values that influence their opinions. Share your own assumptions, values, and opinions. If you cannot find common ground upon which to agree, then agree to disagree.

13. When people insult or criticize you, do not counter in a like manner. Ask them why they feel the way they do. If their feelings are based on a wrong you have done them, apologize and make amends. If they accuse you unjustly, simply deny your guilt and share your feelings about this. If they persist in their criticism, remain silent and walk away.

14. Forgive other people the wrongs they have done you. Hold nothing against anyone. Resentment hurts you more than it does them.

Carrying Your Crosses

There is no true spiritual growth without the cross of Christ. By cross, I mean the inner struggles and difficult circumstances you will experience precisely because you are trying to live a Christian life. When you come to these times, you will feel tempted to give up on the spiritual life, to run away, or to take the easy way out. You will know, however, that to do any of the above will not bring you peace of mind.

It is easy to follow Christ when all is going well. It is also easy to love other people when they are healthy or kind to you or attractive. As Jesus said, even tax collectors and sinners can do this. But what about when all is not going well, when others are sick and ugly, or when people mistreat you? Those are times when the ego-survival values of the false self system emerge with great energy. Yet you know that this is the self that must die for you to experience the life that Christ brings. It is in refusing to indulge the false self by embracing your cross and clinging to Christ that the false self will be put to death. Thus the cross is recognized as the means by which your spiritual life is deepened and purified. This is the great secret of Christianity and the reason why the cross is the symbol of our religion.

This does not mean that carrying the cross is easy! It does mean that your struggles are not in vain; it is worth the effort to persist in living a spiritual life. Many of the saints were so convinced of the transforming power of the cross that they welcomed opposition and struggles with joy.

Simply accepting the difficulties inevitable in living a Christian spiritual life is an excellent way to begin to embrace the cross of Christ. Here are a few additional suggestions:

1. Carrying a cross means that you persist in the effort to love. It does not mean that you must repress your feelings about what is going on in your life. Talk to someone about these struggles. A spiritual director can be a supportive listener while encouraging you to persist in your commitments to love. If you do not process your feelings in a healthy way, you can actually be giving this energy over to the false self system.

2. Carrying a cross does not mean that you must allow another person to abuse you. If it is possible for you to separate from the other during times when they are abusive, then do so.

3. During times of struggle, it is helpful to reflect on why this situation is so difficult for you. The cross reveals us to ourselves, and we usually find that the false self is at the

bottom of our experience of conflict. We have what we don't want, and we want what we don't have. If you can learn this about your attitude, then perhaps you can change those parts of your attitude that are in conflict with love.

4. Pray for the good of the person or situation you are struggling with.

5. Pray for the grace to know and do God's will during this time.

Rhythm for Daily Living

How do you bring everything we've covered in this book into a plan for daily living? This is a very great challenge!

It would be a great mistake—perhaps the greatest of all—to think that living a Christian spiritual life means *doing* all sorts of grand things. Far from it. Spirituality is more concerned with your daily manner of being, from which your doing will follow. The exercises we have encouraged in this book are largely in the service of being, rather than of doing.

Still, there are a few things you must do each day to keep your manner of being centered in the Spirit.

1. *Daily prayer*. I recommend starting your day with twenty to thirty minutes of prayer before you read the newspaper or have any kind of mental input. Even if you are not a "morning person," you will find that giving to God the openness of your "morning mind" enables God to plant spiritual seeds that will grow and bear fruit all day long.

2. *Living in the NOW*. God is here now, loving you and all creation. If you are lost in thoughts about the past or future, you are missing the moment of God. Morning prayer helps you focus on God's loving presence NOW. You can remain in this presence all through the day by calling your attention

back to the present moment, by doing fully whatever it is you're doing, and by keeping your heart open to give and receive love.

3. *Spiritual reading.* Feed yourself good spiritual reading for at least fifteen minutes each day. Learn more about your faith, about spirituality, about growth. This kind of reading is not a substitute for prayer.

4. *Daily examen.* End each day with this spiritual exercise.

I consider these four recommendations to be minimal for anyone who would make the spiritual life a top priority. Even so, there will surely be some who will say that they have no time for prayer or spiritual reading or examen or that these are disciplines more appropriate for professional religious than for laypeople. Such people do not neglect to feed their bodies, however, nor, most likely, to waste hours each day watching television and indulging other worldly, superficial pursuits. If you wish to grow in the Spirit, you must likewise feed your spirit. This is as true for laypeople as for religious.

A few words about television are in order here. Surely, this invention has done far more to change patterns in American family life than anything else in the last thirty years. It has been my observation that the more one grows spiritually, the less one is inclined to watch television—or, if one does watch it, he or she discovers that television (and radio, too, for that matter) is a major source of mental agitation and emotional stimulation, both of which are obstacles to nourishing prayer.

The human brain did not develop in a context of hours and hours of watching television. Consequently, the mind requires hours to unravel the meaning of all the input from a couple of programs and all the commercials. In addition, it seems that television programming plays to the least common denominators in intelligence and values. Educational programming and a few weekly series are exceptions, but in general, mental and spiritual life will be greatly weakened in one who watches hours of television each day.

As you consider developing a daily rhythm for growing in the Spirit, then, you should examine the role of television and radio in your life. If you spend hours watching television each day, would you be willing to reduce this time in exchange for deepening your spiritual growth or volunteering your services in some manner? The results will amaze you!

Considering all of the foregoing, draw up your own plan for daily living. Talk about it with your spiritual directors and evaluate it from time to time to discern what is the best way for you to live. What works at one time in life might not work during another. The spiritual life is always growing and changing, and you must adapt yourself accordingly.

Appendix One
· · · · · · · · · · · · · · · · · ·

The Method of
Centering Prayer

Thomas Keating

Theological Background: The grace of Pentecost affirms that the risen Jesus is among us as the glorified Christ. Christ lives in each of us as the Enlightened One, present everywhere and at all times. He is the living Master who continuously sends the Holy Spirit to dwell within us and to bear witness to his Resurrection by empowering us to experience and manifest the fruits of the Spirit and the Beatitudes both in prayer and action.

Lectio Divina: Lectio Divina is the most traditional way of cultivating friendship with Christ. It is a way of listening to the texts of scripture as if we were in conversation with Christ and he were suggesting the topics of conversation. The daily encounter with Christ and reflection on his word leads beyond mere acquaintanceship to an attitude of friendship, trust and love. Conversation simplifies and gives way to communing, or as Gregory the Great (sixth century), summarizing the Christian contemplative tradition, put it, "resting in God." This was the classical meaning of contemplative prayer for the first sixteen centuries.

Contemplative Prayer: Contemplative Prayer is the normal development of the grace of baptism and the regular practice of *Lectio Divina*. We may think of prayer as thoughts or feelings expressed in words. But this is only one expression. Contemplative Prayer is the opening of mind and heart—our whole being—to God, the Ultimate Mystery, beyond thoughts, words, and emotions. We open our awareness to God whom we know by faith is within us, closer than breathing, closer than thinking, closer than choosing—closer than consciousness itself. Contemplative Prayer is a process of interior purification leading, if we consent, to divine union.

The Method of Centering Prayer: Centering Prayer is a method designed to facilitate the development of contemplative prayer by preparing our faculties to cooperate with this gift. It is an attempt to present the teaching of earlier times (e.g., *The Cloud of Unknowing*) in an updated form and to put a certain order and regularity into it. It is not meant to replace other kinds of prayer; it simply puts other kinds of prayer into a new and fuller perspective. During the time of prayer we consent to God's presence and action within. At other times our attention moves outward to discover God's presence everywhere.

What Centering Prayer Is Not

  a. It is not a technique.
  b. It is not a relaxation exercise.
  c. It is not a form of self-hypnosis.
  d. It is not a charismatic gift.
  e. It is not a parapsychological phenomenon.
  f. It is not limited to the "felt" presence of God.
  g. It is not discursive meditation or affective prayer.

Explanation of the Guidelines for Centering Prayer

  I. *"Choose a sacred word as the symbol of your intention to consent to God's presence and action within."*

1. The sacred word expresses our intention to be in God's presence and to yield to the divine action.
2. The sacred word should be chosen during a brief period of prayer, asking the Holy Spirit to inspire us with one that is especially suitable for us. (Examples: Lord, Jesus, *Abba*, Father, Mother, Love...Peace, Shalom.)
3. Having chosen a sacred word, we do not change it during the prayer period, for that would be to start thinking again.
4. A simple inward gaze upon God may be more suitable for some persons than the sacred word. In this case, one consents to God's presence and action by turning inwardly toward God as if gazing upon him. The same guidelines apply to the sacred gaze as to the sacred word.

II. *"Sitting comfortably and with eyes closed, settle briefly, and silently introduce the sacred word as the symbol of your consent to God's presence and action within."*

1. By "sitting comfortably" is meant relatively comfortably; not so comfortably that we encourage sleep, but sitting comfortably enough to avoid thinking about the discomfort of our bodies during this time of prayer.
2. Whatever sitting position we choose, we keep the back straight.
3. If we fall asleep, we continue the prayer for a few minutes upon awakening, if we can spare the time.
4. Praying in this way after a main meal encourages drowsiness. Better to wait an hour at least before Centering Prayer. Praying in this way just before retiring may disturb one's sleep pattern.
5. We close our eyes to let go of what is going on around and within us.
6. We introduce the sacred word inwardly and as gently as laying a feather on a piece of absorbent cotton.

III. *"When you become aware of thoughts, return ever-so-gently to the sacred word."*

1. "Thoughts" is an umbrella term for every perception including sense perceptions, feelings, images, memories, reflections, and commentaries.
2 Thoughts are a normal part of Centering Prayer.
3. By "returning ever-so-gently to the sacred word," a minimum of effort is indicated. This is the only activity we initiate during the time of Centering Prayer.
4. During the course of our prayer, the sacred word may become vague or even disappear.

IV. *"At the end of the prayer period, remain in silence with eyes closed for two or three minutes."*

1. If this prayer is done in a group, the leader may slowly recite the Our Father during the additional two or three minutes while others listen.
2. The additional two or three minutes give the psyche time to readjust to the external senses and enable us to bring the atmosphere of silence into daily life.

Some Practical Points
1. The minimum time for this prayer is twenty minutes. Two periods are recommended each day, one first thing in the morning and one in the afternoon or early evening.
2. The end of the prayer period can be indicated by a timer, provided it does not have an audible tick or loud sound when it goes off.
3. The principal effects of Centering Prayer are experienced in daily life, not in the period of Centering Prayer itself.
4. Physical Symptoms:
   a. We may notice slight pains, itches, or twitches in various

parts of the body or a generalized restlessness. These are usually due to the untying of emotional knots in the body.

b. We may also notice heaviness or lightness in the extremities. This is usually due to a deep level of spiritual attentiveness.

c. In either case, we pay no attention, or we allow the mind to rest briefly on the sensation and then return to the sacred word.

5. *Lectio Divina* provides the conceptual background for the development of Centering Prayer.

6. A support group praying and sharing together once a week helps maintain one's commitment to the prayer.

Some Points for Further Development

1. During the prayer period, various kinds of thoughts may be distinguished (cf., *Open Mind, Open Heart,* chapters 6-10).

a. Ordinary wanderings of the imagination or memory.

b. Thoughts that give rise to attractions or aversions.

c. Insights and psychological breakthroughs.

d. Self-reflections such as "How am I doing?" or "This peace is just great!"

e. Thoughts that arise from the unloading of the unconscious.

2. During this prayer we avoid analyzing our experience, harboring expectations or aiming at some specific goal such as:

a. Repeating the sacred word continuously.

b. Having no thoughts.

c. Making the mind a blank.

d. Feeling peaceful or consoled.

e. Achieving a spiritual experience.

For more information and resources concerning Centering Prayer, contact Contemplative Outreach, Ltd., 9 William Street, P.O. Box 737, Butler, NJ 07405. Phone Number (201) 838-3384.

Appendix Two
· · · · · · · · · · · · · · · · · · · ·

On Making
a Retreat*

Life is busy and noisy for many of us. If we are not careful, we will lose touch with ourselves and fall prey to fragmentation and dissipation. To remain whole and "in touch," we need to take time each day to let go of our busy-ness and be still with God. We also need to "keep holy the Sabbath," which is why the Church forbids any unnecessary servile work on Sundays. On the positive side, we can also "go to Mass, visit our families, and laze around." In a culture that ultimately traces the value of everything to dollars and cents, this taking time each day for prayer and giving our Sundays to the Lord is a most countercultural stance.

Making a retreat takes this stance a step further. On a retreat we are giving up several (or many) days to give attention to our spiritual life. We are leaving our ordinary everyday environments and going off to another place to focus on our relationship with God. We have our precedent for doing this in the example of Jesus and his disciples. (See Mark 6:31.) Things are no different now than they were then. Now, we are the disciples, and he calls us to leave our busy-ness behind for a while to spend time with him.

Types of Retreats: But what exactly is a retreat? What goes on there? Twenty years ago these questions would have been easy to answer. At that time there were basically two types of retreats, silent-directed and silent-preached. The latter also included times for the rosary, the Way of the Cross, and other devotionals.

Glancing through the offerings of retreat centers today, however, you will find many additional possibilities (many centers no longer even offer silent-directed or silent-preached retreats). Many creative and effective models for retreats have been developed and popularized during the past twenty years. As a result of this virtual explosion in retreat innovation, more choices are available to people than ever before. If you wish to "come away and rest for a while," there are many ways to do so. The type of retreat you choose to attend will depend largely on what you perceive your needs to be at a particular time in your life.

Here are some broad, general categories of retreats:

1. *Directed.* A directed retreat will usually be from three to thirty days, using the Spiritual Exercises of Saint Ignatius of Loyola. Silence is observed, except during Mass and the daily meeting with the director. Three to five prayer periods a day are recommended.
2. *Private.* In a private retreat, you simply pay room and board to a retreat center, using the time and place to "get away from it all." You design your own schedule for prayer and silence and plug into the center's schedule for Mass and meals.
3. *Preached.* The usual timespan for a preached retreat is three to five days, with two preached conferences each day, generally developing a theme through the retreat. Between conferences, there may be times for silence, Mass, individual sessions, and unstructured times. Traditional formats will also include times for rosary, the Way of the Cross, and other devotionals.

4. *Guided*. This type of retreat usually lasts three to eight days, with one preached conference per day, individual sessions, and silence.

5. *Group dynamic*. This retreat format is usually offered over a weekend and includes several talks, times for discussion, group activities, Eucharist, and reconciliation. The awakening of faith in the context of community is emphasized. Cursillo, Marriage Encounter, Engaged Encounter, Beginning Experience, Teens Encounter Christ, Awakening, Search, Parish Renewal, and other popular retreat programs are examples of this format.

6. *Charismatic*. Times for teaching, praise, fellowship, and Mass, generally in a large-group context, characterize charismatic retreats. Their distinctive feature is the emphasis on praise and the manifestation of the gifts of the Spirit in building community. These are usually weekend retreats.

7. *Contemplative*. A contemplative retreat will last from three to ten days, usually including brief periods of teaching or instruction, individual sessions, and several periods a day for sitting quietly in God's loving presence. Retreats on centering prayer and Zen retreats belong to this type.

8. *Twelve Steps*. This type of retreat is a combination of the preached and group dynamic formats, usually held over a weekend. In addition to conferences, there is time for Twelve Step meetings.

9. *Specialty*. Some retreats may fit none of the above categories. Instead, they develop a specific theme using teachings, quiet periods, work sheets, group discussion, and other dynamics. Retreats on Myers-Briggs, Enneagram, Healing the Child Within, journaling, male spirituality, female spirituality, yoga, Creation spirituality, wellness, and many other topics can be found in the offerings of retreat centers today. These may last from a weekend to a week and usually feature a speaker with expertise in the theme being emphasized.

What kind of retreat is right for you? Ideally, this is a question that your spiritual director/companion could help you answer. If you have no such help in your life, then I encourage you to find someone. In the meantime, however, the best way to decide is to read through the offerings of retreat centers in your area and see what interests you. If you feel moved to attend a particular retreat, ask the Holy Spirit to confirm this for you in some manner—maybe by simply giving you the conviction that this is what you need at this time in your life. Generally, the retreats that look interesting to you will be retreats that address some of your needs.

Once you make your decision, you must register with the center. I mention this obvious fact because too often people put this off until the last minute only to discover to their disappointment that the retreat has been filled. So get out your checkbook and register as soon as you know what you want to do. It is impossible to register too early for a retreat.

Make the Most of It: If I could recommend one thing to people, it would be that *you be open to what the Lord wants to tell you or show you during the retreat.* We spend much of our time telling God, ourselves, and other people who we think we are. On a retreat it is time to listen to what God has to say about who you are.

A retreat is a special and blessed time! If you are open to the retreat process, the Lord can accomplish more with you during even a relatively brief retreat than during months of ordinary, everyday growth. I have experienced this time and again with myself and have talked with others who have had the same experience in retreats through the years.

Frequently, expectations people bring to the retreat prevent this experience from happening. Many come expecting a certain thing to happen to them and refuse to let go of this expectation even when it becomes clear that God has something else in mind.

In other words, your own preconceptions about what *should* be happening to you on the retreat often place an obstacle in the way of your receiving fully what God has to offer you.

No doubt, however, you will spend some time telling God how you think and feel about things during the retreat. While some retreat formats encourage this, they all encourage you also at some time to *listen* to what God has to say to you. This listening may come through Scripture, through a talk, through a memory, through a journal exercise—there are many ways it can happen. If you are open to it and praying for it, God will let you know this during the retreat. Such knowledge is worth every penny you invest in the retreat and every bit of pain you experience in coming to the knowledge. For, in the end, who we really are has nothing to do with our own ideas but with God's view of us. And *God's* view, we learn, is generally more honest, loving, and freeing than our own.

It is this kind of knowledge that a retreat invites us to experience. It is this kind of knowledge that we truly hunger for.

* This article originally appeared in a slightly different form under the title "So Our Souls Can Catch Up" in *Praying* magazine, January-February 1993.

Appendix Three

The Gifts of the
Holy Spirit

Traditional Catholic spirituality has viewed spiritual growth in terms of an increase in the gifts of the Holy Spirit. These gifts are graces that enable the individual to live a holy life; indeed, they are a perfect description of holiness. They are obtained through prayer and sacrament but sustained through living a life of love and service, which the gifts make possible.

The Infused Gifts
(Isaiah 11:2, 3)

1. *Wisdom.* The integration of divine truth into everyday life.
2. *Understanding.* The ability of the soul to grasp divine truth.
3. *Knowledge.* Ability to judge things in the light of faith.
4. *Fortitude.* Courage. Strength of will to live according to God's plan.
5. *Counsel.* Enables one to make good decisions. Discernment.
6. *Piety.* Produces a love of God.
7. *Fear of God.* Profound respect for the justice and majesty of God.

The Charismatic Gifts
(1 Corinthians 12 and other sources)

These are considered preternatural gifts in that they are manifestations of extrasensory powers under the guidance of the Holy Spirit for the building up of the Church. As such, these gifts do not indicate any special quality of holiness (as do the infused gifts), but they can be helps to holiness.

1. *Prophecy.* To hear a message from God and speak it.
2. *Healing.* To communicate healing power to another in need.
3. *Knowledge.* To know the secret thoughts, memories, feelings, or desires of another.
4. *Visionaries.* To know the future or what's going on in another place at this time.
5. *Inspired preaching.* To expound on God's Word in such a manner as to deeply inspire and motivate others.
6. *Glossolalia.* To speak in an unknown language for purposes of giving praise to God or as a prelude to prophecy.

The Fruits of the Holy Spirit: In addition to the infused gifts of the Spirit, mystical theology has listed various fruits of the Holy Spirit as evidence of spiritual growth. These are mentioned in Galatians 5:22-23, where they are contrasted with the fruits of self-indulgence. The fruits of the Holy Spirit are *love, joy, peace, patience, kindness, generosity, faithfulness, gentleness, self-control.*

Appendix Four
· · · · · · · · · · · · · · · · · · ·

The Gift of Tongues
(Glossolalia)

Speaking in tongues is generally associated with charismatic, or pentecostal, spirituality, although it may be found outside of these forms of worship. In Scripture and in pentecostal communities, it seems to manifest in three distinct ways.

1. The person praying in an unknown language is actually speaking a human language that another person can understand. This is very rare, but it may have been the kind of tongue-speaking mentioned in the Acts of the Apostles 2:3-12.

2. The person praying in tongues is speaking syllables that constitute no known human language but that serve as a catalyst to open this person or another to a prophetic message from God. This is what Saint Paul encourages in 1 Corinthians 14:13-19. Tongue-speaking for purposes of prophetic enrichment can be noted at most charismatic/pentecostal prayer meetings.

3. The purpose of this prayer is the inner healing and spiritual edification of the individual praying. Such tongue-speaking is often called a *prayer language*. It may manifest spontaneously during prayer times and throughout the day. This

impulse to pray in tongues may be suppressed, or the individual may choose to pray silently or aloud. We read of this type of prayer in many places in Scripture. (See, for example, Romans 8:26-27 and 1 Corinthians 14:1-2, 18-19.)

My concern in this appendix is with the third kind of tongue-speaking, prayer language. From my own experience, I am convinced of the value of this type of prayer. The impulse for it seems to come from the Holy Spirit through unconscious dimensions of the psyche. Its consequences are inner peace, healing of emotions, and awakening the soul to the presence of God. It is also a natural bridge between active, mental prayer and quiet, contemplative prayer. Obviously, there are many Christians who could benefit from growth in these fruits, and this is why I encourage this form of prayer.

One need not be a practicing member of a pentecostal prayer group to receive this gift (although a Life in the Spirit Seminar in a Catholic charismatic group can serve as an excellent introduction to it). The prayer-language manifestation of glossolalia is for the individual's own edification, while the other types are for the community's growth. Because the prayer language is for the spiritual growth of the individual, I believe this particular manifestation of glossolalia is available to *all* Christians. The other manifestations of glossolalia, as with the other charismatic gifts, may be available to only a few and then at only certain times and in special circumstances.

Receiving Glossolalia as Prayer Language: Because the prayer language generally manifests and grows in a context of praising God, it is frequently observed in pentecostal worship, where the praise of God is the primary focus of the group. But anyone may praise God at any time. Indeed, the praise of God is a marvelous way to love God with your whole heart, whole soul, whole mind, and whole strength.

In their excellent book on Christian prayer and commitment, *Friendship With Jesus* (Dove Publications, 1974), Joseph Lange, OSFS, and Anthony Cushing suggest the following approach to asking for and receiving the gift of tongues:

"Step 1. To receive the gift of tongues, begin by relaxing. It is not something you can do for yourself, so there is no point in becoming all worked up trying to get it. You don't get it, you *receive* it. Find the most relaxing place and position you can. One person I know received it in the bathtub!

"Step 2. Enter into God's presence. Focus your attention on the presence of Jesus, the giver of the gift. We do not baptize in the Spirit. We do not give the gifts. Jesus does. Focus on his presence. Remember his perfect love for you.

"Step 3. Ask Him to stir up the Spirit within you, to pour out His Spirit upon you, to fill you up so that it rushes out of you in this new language of prayer.

"Step 4. Open your mouth and speak out, your mind and heart on him. Speak out in anything but your native language. Let the Spirit form the language, the syllables. Praise him."

If, after a few minutes, Jesus has not given you this gift, switch to your native language and give praise to him. Be silent for a while. Talk to him again and try again. Be persevering but don't be excessive. If you don't receive it, try again another time and follow the advice we gave above.

"Praise God, the giver of all good gifts."

Appendix Five

· · · · · · · · · · · · · · · · · · ·

The Nature
of the Soul

Although the Christian spiritual journey is primarily focused on the relationship between a person and God, it is helpful to have a Christian understanding of the nature of the soul. This is especially desirable today when many people are attracted to Eastern or metaphysical views of human nature that are at odds with Christianity. Many seem to be unaware that Christianity, too, has come to a deep and comprehensive metaphysical understanding of human nature. This understanding can help us make sense of the true meaning of spirituality.

The Christian View of the Soul: The following points should not be taken as a summary of Christian metaphysics but simply as a listing of some of the distinctive features of the Christian view of the soul.

1. The soul is a spiritual reality oriented toward animating matter to form a body. With other spirits, it shares these characteristics:
   a. *Simplicity*. The soul is one indivisible whole with no parts. It contains the physical body, which it informs to

the smallest atom to make the body live. It also contains faculties of reason, will, memory, and so forth; but these are not divisions of the soul—only faculties to enable its operations.

b. *Immortality*. Other life forms are said to have a vegetative soul (plant life, animal physiology) and/or animal soul (life of the senses, instinctive reactions). These souls are perishable. The spiritual soul of a human being contains the vegetative and animal souls and is responsible for their existence and functioning. At death, however, the vegetative and animal levels cease to exist in a human being, since they are fundamentally oriented to the life of the physical body, which is left behind at death.

c. *Immateriality*. The soul is a spiritual substance, and as such, it is immortal. Nevertheless, it is a spirit that is meant to give life to a physical body and to exercise itself in a body.

d. *Freedom*. The soul may choose to do this or that. These choices are limited by the information available.

e. *Intelligence*. Like angels, the soul is capable of grasping spiritual truth directly through intuition. It may also gain knowledge through the exercise of reason from information obtained from the senses.

f. *Personal*. Each soul is individual, belonging to the individual, whose intellectual and volitional experiences are possessed by that individual. This characteristic is responsible for the experience of self-consciousness.

g. *Creatureliness*. The soul is a creation of God. It is not eternal; it is created directly by God at conception. Therefore, the soul is not a divine substance, although it is dependent on God for its existence and is therefore connected with God because of the fact of its existence.

2. Without a body, the spiritual soul is metaphysically deficient, for the intelligence and exercising of the characteristics of the soul described above are oriented toward life in a body. This is why a complete restoration of the soul calls for a body in and through which the soul may express itself. A human soul differs from an angelic spirit in this regard, for an angelic spirit is created to know and express itself in a purely spiritual state of being.

3. When the spiritual soul was first given, its contact with the Divine was such that its energy was infused with divine energy so that the animal, vegetative, and physical levels were taken up into the immortality of the spiritual soul. With the Fall, however, the soul maintained its spiritual nature, but its energy was no longer infused with the divine energy. Consequentially, the body lost the immortality infused by the spiritual soul and became destined for death.

4. As a spirit, the soul may live apart from the body in the afterlife. This is called the intermediate state of the soul. During this phase of its journey, the soul experiences all of the qualities of spirits listed above. So the soul intuitively comprehends its relationship with God and others, thus entering into either hell, purgatory, or heaven.

5. Although the usual manner of knowing for the soul is through the body and information gained from the senses, it is nonetheless possible for the embodied soul to experience its spiritual nature while in the body. Thus it is that philosophers sometimes speak of two experiences of the soul:

    a. The *corporal soul*. The normal state of the soul in this life. Its rational and intuitive intelligence is ultimately derived from sensory information and directed toward actions to be performed by the body.

    b. *The partly body-free soul*. As a spirit, the soul is not completely contained by the life and needs of the body. It reaches beyond the body and may experience some of the qualities of a pure spirit, although imperfectly. The partly body-free soul explains phenomena such as extrasensory perception, cosmic consciousness, spiritual travel (astral body travel), occult phenomena, and natural mysticism (for example, some form of Eastern spirituality).

Certain ascetical practices can loosen the hold of the soul on the physical body so that it may experience its spiritual nature in this manner.

In this state, the soul may realize its connection with God as the giver of existence and so obtain a kind of natural, nonpersonal union with God. This seems to be the kind of experience that practitioners of certain Eastern and New Age spiritualities tend toward. Such spiritualities have explored the powers of the soul and lead their adherents, through a life of moral living and ascetical discipline, to realize this natural union between the soul and its Maker. This natural, or metaphysical, mysticism is obviously different from the relational spirituality described in this book and in the Judeo-Christian tradition, although it is certainly not without merit and should by no means be considered diabolical.

In this state, too, the soul may sometimes communicate with angelic, demonic, and disembodied spirits, who may in turn communicate to the physical realm through the faculties of the spiritual soul. This is the basis for channeling (necromancy) and spiritualism, both of which are condemned by the Church, since it is unlikely that good spirits would be involved in such communications. This may also explain some of the dynamics of demonic possession.

It frequently happens that a Christian mystic, too, will be drawn to this state, wherein the soul will enjoy ecstatic union with God or receive communication from God without going through the usual channels of sensation and conceptualization.

This is called *infused contemplation*, a deep union of love between God and the soul made possible by grace.

The partly body-free soul may also explain manifestations of extrasensory preternatural powers. Such powers need not be attributed to angels, demons, or disembodied spirits but may belong to the soul itself. Generally, these powers lie dormant in the unconscious or superconscious mind. In the partly body-free state, however, they may manifest in certain individuals. This explanation accounts for the unpredictability of these gifts and the inability of the person to produce them at will.

6. As a created spirit, the soul naturally longs for union with its maker even while it infuses life into the body. The fundamental dispositions of the soul, then, are twofold:

    a. To give life to the body and thus cultivate its spiritual powers in a context of embodied life to which the soul is properly suited (unlike angels and demons, which are not suited for embodiment).

    b. To be united with God, its source of life and existence. Catholic theology does not see an opposition between these two dispositions. The body and its needs do not negate the spiritual life of the soul. The body is not a prison of the soul nor an obstacle to union with God. Nevertheless, a soul too attached to bodily life cannot be united with God nor can a soul who rejects the life of the body. A sound spiritual approach recognizes the importance of proper and disciplined care for the body and its needs while cultivating union with God.

Appendix Six

. . . .

Stages of Growth
in Christian Prayer

One way to chart the spiritual journey is to follow its development through various stages of prayer. These stages are described below. They seem to apply to most people, although there are many exceptions to this general pattern.

Active Prayer: Sometimes called *discursive prayer*, active prayer includes all forms of prayer that we initiate through the use of our mental faculties (such as thinking, reasoning, imagining, acts of will, visualization, remembering). Following is a typical description of progression in active prayer.

- *Sacred reading*
- *Meditation on the reading:* intellectual and imaginative reflection. Recognizing and applying principles. Resolutions.
- *Affective prayer:* petitions, thanksgiving, intercession, remorse, praise, adoration.
- *Simplicity, simple regard, centering prayer:* this usually follows affective prayer and consists of simple acts of the will to focus lovingly on God and to give God consent to live and act in the soul.

Infused Prayer: This is contemplative prayer, properly speaking. Here the soul is embraced by God without exercising the faculties. God communicates Spirit-to-spirit, as it were. Generally, contemplative prayer begins as a natural development from the life of active prayer, which helps to prepare the faculties of the soul to receive the gift of contemplation. It should be known that the stages of contemplative union described below refer not only to experiences during times of prayer but also to times when one is not in formal prayer. They are states of being rather than prayer experiences, per se.

- *Prayer of quiet.* God is united with the deeper levels of the will, but the faculties of thinking, imagination, and sensation remain untouched by this contemplation and often roam about freely. Nevertheless, one is aware of being embraced by God.
- *Prayer of union.* The union between the soul and God includes the mental and sensual faculties, which rest quietly during this prayer. In this beautiful state, one experiences the certitude of God's presence and is delivered from weariness and tedium. God refreshes the soul so completely that one scarcely experiences the need for sleep and would prefer to spend time resting in union with God. There is no loss of conscious awareness in this prayer.
- *Prayer of ecstatic union.* Many, but not all, Christian mystics evidence this state. In ecstasy, the soul is so completely united with God that all self-awareness is lost, along with sensory awareness and consciousness of space and time. The activities of the corporal soul are diminished so that the soul, in a partly body-free state, may more fully contemplate the love and beauty of God. The consequences of this prayer are many, including deep inner healing and great virtue. It should

be known, however, that there are other experiences of ecstasy besides contemplative ones. Psychic and occult ecstasies may also be found. The mere fact of ecstasy is no indication of mystical contemplation or holiness.

- *Transforming union.* There is no longer any obstacle in the soul to receiving the graces of God, so life proceeds in full union between the soul and God. All the faculties are trained to cooperate with the Holy Spirit, and in turn they are infused with the loving energies of the Spirit to function according to the will of God. Now something of an "ordinary state" returns, although one is never without the immediate experience of God's loving presence. The soul continues to learn and grow but in full union with God. This is the fully liberated soul, that already enjoys something of the wonder of heaven while on this earth. Sin is still a possibility but is generally avoided.

Transition From Active Prayer to Infused Contemplation: As already noted, one begins the spiritual journey by practicing active forms of prayer, and contemplative prayer eventually emerges spontaneously. In describing this transition from active to contemplative prayer, Saint John of the Cross gives three signs to validate this experience. These signs are paraphrased below:

1. One no longer seems to gain any sense of closeness to God through the practice of active prayer.
2. One is not sick nor lukewarm in faith nor in sin but is still drawn to spirituality and desirous of spiritual growth.
3. One enjoys being in God's presence in general loving awareness, without any particular discursive knowledge or awareness.

The first two signs indicate that one is no longer growing through the practice of active prayer forms but that this is not due to spiritual neglect or lack of discipline. The third sign, however, indicates the actual beginnings of contemplation, probably as the prayer of quiet. Saint John encourages one in this situation to diminish the amount of time spent in active prayer and to enjoy the general, loving awareness of God.

It may happen that some experience the first two signs but not the third. What should one in this situation do? The answer is to continue to live a life of faith and love, praying as best you can. A regular practice of centering prayer can help prepare you to receive the gift of contemplation, but a much better preparation comes from your efforts to love other people. Contemplation is a union of love between God and the soul that overflows to the intellectual and sensual faculties. Therefore, love (not knowledge or ascetical practices) is the best preparation for contemplation, and the best way to live, at any rate. A saint is not judged according to the degree of contemplative prayer evidenced but according to the love he or she has shown.

Dark Nights of the Soul: During the process of spiritual growth, one goes through many changes as a direct result of the deepening union between God and the soul. Saint John of the Cross spoke of these transformational experiences as *Dark Nights of the Soul*. They are called Dark Nights because the light of God pouring into the soul is of such brilliance and purity that the soul cannot fully perceive it, so it seems to be a "dark light." Also, this light illuminates all the hidden and dark energies of the soul, bringing to awareness one's sinfulness and poverty of spirit.

Two Dark Nights are usually recognized, although some authors describe more. These Nights are general descriptions of the spiritual transformation process. Some people can identify with these Nights; others who are obviously progressing seem to experience very few of these characteristics. Each person is unique, and so is each journey. Nevertheless, a knowledge of the Dark Nights may help some to better name, validate, and accept their experiences. It is with these ends in mind that I include the following brief descriptions of the two Dark Nights of Saint John of the Cross.

1. *Night of the Senses.* Almost all who make a serious commitment to prayer will come upon this Night within a few months to a couple of years, according to Saint John. This Night generally signals the transition from active to contemplative prayer and is characterized by the three signs listed above. With the beginnings of contemplative prayer, one may experience deep emotional pains that had been repressed. Depression and neurotic tendencies may also surface as the Spirit works with the emotional level of the soul to cleanse it of pain and enable it to give and receive love more freely. There is a certain serenity and even joy along with these pains, which encourages one to persist in this Night and which distinguishes these pains from psychopathologies not related to spiritual growth. Generally, this Night lasts several months to two years. Its fruit is emotional healing, love of God, deepening contemplation, and a new ego structure better adapted to life in the Spirit. Because of the pains of this Night, however, many turn away from the spiritual journey at this point, and enter into a period of complacency regarding their spiritual needs.

2. *Night of the Spirit.* Those courageous souls who have been through the Night of the Senses may eventually be led into this Night. Here the deepest roots of one's unhealthy attitudes are uprooted and cleansed. Indeed, the entire rational and volitional life is thoroughly cleansed of all that is incompatible with life in the Spirit. This Night brings total liberation from the tyranny of the false self and establishes one in Transforming Union. Such

excellent fruit, however, cannot be tasted without going through the mental anguish and energy upheavals that characterize this Night. In many ways, however, it is not as emotionally painful as the Night of the Senses, for the former Night brought peace and stability to the emotional levels. According to Saint John, this Night is purgatory on earth. Those souls who do not undergo this Night on earth will have to do so in the afterlife—unless they are bound for hell, of course. After going through this Night, which may last for years, the soul experiences something of the joys of heaven while on this earth. The energies of the soul are thoroughly infused with the loving energies of the Spirit so that the soul manifests the gifts of the Holy Spirit in abundance.

Note: For a recent comprehensive discussion of the Nights, see *Invitation to Love: The Way of Christian Contemplation,* by Thomas Keating (Element Books, 1992). Father Keating calls these Nights the Divine Therapy, for they heal the soul more completely than any human psychotherapy could possibly hope to accomplish.

Suggested Reading

Arraj, James. *The Inner Nature of Faith: A Mysterious Knowledge Coming Through the Heart*. Chiloquin, OR: Inner Growth Books, 1988.

de Mello, Anthony, S.J. *Awareness: A De Mello Spirituality Conference in His Own Words*. New York: Doubleday, 1990.

Greene, Thomas. *When the Well Runs Dry: Prayer Beyond the Beginnings*. Notre Dame, IN: Ave Maria Press, 1979.

Keating, Thomas. *Open Mind, Open Heart: The Contemplative Dimension of the Gospel*. Rockport, MA: Element Books, 1991.

_____. *Invitation to Love*. Rockport, MA: Element Books, 1992.

Lange, Joseph and Anthony Cushing. *Friendship With Jesus*. Pecos, NM: Dove Publications, 1974.

May, Gerald. *Will and Spirit*. San Francisco: Harper and Row, 1987.

_____. *Addiction and Grace: Love and Spirituality in the Healing of Addictions*. San Francisco: Harper and Row, 1988.

Schaef, Anne Wilson. *When Society Becomes an Addict*. San Francisco: Harper and Row, 1987.

St. Teresa of Avila. *The Interior Castle*. New York: Doubleday, 1972.

Tugwell, Simon, O.P. *Ways of Imperfection.* Springfield, IL: Templegate, 1985.

Woods, Richard. *Christian Spirituality.* Chicago: Thomas More Press, 1989.

The above books are not available from Liguori Publications. Order from your local bookstore.

Also by Philip St. Romain

Books

Twelve Steps to Spiritual Wholeness: A Christian Pathway ($3.95)

Freedom From Codependency ($3.95)

Pathways to Serenity ($5.95)

Audios

Twelve Steps to Spiritual Wholeness. 2 tapes. ($14.95)

Codependency ($14.95)

Basics of Spirituality ($14.95)

Order from your local bookstore or write to

Liguori Publications

Box 060, Liguori, MO 63057-9999

(Please add $3 for postage and handling for orders under $9.99; $3 for orders between $10 and $14.99; $4 for orders over $15.)